RETIRE
FASTER
SMARTER
RICHER

MICHAELA CAVALLARO

CENTENNIAL BOOKS

RETIRE
FASTER
SMARTER
RICHER

Table of Contents

22

58

128

Discover the Freedom of Early Retirement
Leaving the Workforce Behind Looks Much Different for Today's Active Retirees

Now more than ever, retirement is what you make of it. Gone are the days when you retire on your 65th birthday, get a home on a golf course and ride out your days playing bridge and sipping iced tea, living off the pension you collect from the company you've worked for your entire life. Today's retirees are a dynamic bunch. They're climbing mountains, running marathons and taking classes to learn new skills. They're both younger and older: On the one hand, it's no longer uncommon to retire at 55 (or even earlier), and on the other hand, life spans are increasing. Retirees are working part time both to earn more money, and because they enjoy it. And they're relying on self-funded retirement plans rather than company pensions.

These changes have brought a greater sense of freedom to retirement—but they can also bring confusion and unease. There was a comfort to having retirement defined for you, even if that definition was relatively narrow. Defining retirement for yourself means navigating your way through seemingly endless options, a process that can be intimidating—even overwhelming—without a road map to guide you.

This book aims to be that road map. We start by providing an overview of the new retirement, with a particular focus on retiring early—how to do it, when to do it and whether it's right for you. We also discuss housing issues, from downsizing to tax considerations to the pros and cons of retiring abroad (Bali, anyone?). We take a deep dive into the ever-shifting and sometimes bewildering world of health care, including health insurance options, how to pay for prescription drugs and how much you can expect to spend on medical care over the course of your life. Finally, we'll dig into the financial nitty-gritty, with advice on how to grow your savings, deal with debt and invest with confidence. You'll also find guidance on how to balance multiple sources of income, from retirement-account distributions to Social Security checks to annuities to part-time employment.

Whether you're sticking close to home or laying new tracks, your retirement future is limitless.

As you build your vision of your retirement—which may not resemble that of your parents, your friends or your neighbors very closely—keep in mind that retirement isn't really a destination, it's a process. Interests may come and go, circumstances change—and life (as the coronavirus pandemic clearly demonstrated) is constantly throwing curveballs at us. Planning for retirement means preparing for a phase of life that's as fluid—and exciting—as any other you will face. The more you learn, the better equipped you'll be to forge a path of comfort, connection and joy.

— *Michaela Cavallaro*

Retiring Early: What It Takes

Understanding the possibilities of opting out of the workforce—and avoiding the pitfalls

Defining the New Retirement
Financial Independence, Partial Retirement, Digital Nomads and More

The face of retirement is changing. The stereotypical retiree was once an elderly man who whiled away his afternoons on the golf course. Today's retiree might be a 55-year-old who invested wisely and is now enjoying the low cost of living in a Mexican beach town, or a former executive who finally has the time to start the small business she's always dreamed of opening.

This new version of retirement has been driven by a number of social, economic and technological changes. For one, 21st-century retirees are more active and independent than their predecessors. Thanks to improved medical care, they have longer life spans and stay physically fit longer. And because of technological advances, they're also able to enjoy a more mobile retirement. When traveling becomes practical again, retirement may look like roaming the country in an RV or wintering in Central America. In short: This is not your grandparents' retirement.

The New Retirement Is...
Financially Independent

The decline of the traditional pension plan means that today's retirees are increasingly responsible for supporting their own retirement. Fortunately, strategic planning and smart savings are allowing working Americans to fund their own retirement and, in some cases, to leave the working world behind before the typical retirement age of 65 years.

According to the Bureau of Labor Statistics, individuals' average annual expenses peak between the ages of 45 to 54 and then start declining. By trimming expenses and finding ways to live on less, you can stretch your retirement savings further—or retire earlier. For some of today's retirees, that may mean embracing partial retirement or taking on a new part-time

PRO TIP

If you start trimming your expenses now, you can grow a bigger nest egg and ensure your savings will last through a long retirement.

Early retirement can mean devoting more time and energy to staying active.

freelance job. Some people embrace the frugal lifestyle movement, while others relocate to a place that has a lower cost of living.

The New Retirement Is…Employed

Just because you've entered retirement doesn't mean you've given up on working forever. In fact, before widespread shelter-in-place orders slowed down the economy, labor force participation among those 65 and older reached 20 percent, and it's expected to continue to rise in the long run. (In 2002, only 13 percent of this age group was working.)

This rising figure is due in part to the fact that these days many people don't definitively leave the working world behind when they retire. Increasingly, retirement is looking more like a slow phasing out of work rather than a hard

11

Early retirement
can free up plenty
of time for travel.

stop. What that means depends on an individual's situation, of course. It might look like scaling back to part time, taking on consulting work at a former job or working seasonally. Some retirees take a work sabbatical lasting from a few months to a few years before reentering the workforce in some capacity, while others use their newfound freedom to start the small business they've always daydreamed about. Others take on freelance work—as photographers, programmers or graphic designers—to help pay the bills while also staying mentally active.

And it's not just the extra cash that motivates retirees to keep one foot in the working world. According to an AARP survey, one in five retirement-age workers says that job enjoyment is the main reason they keep working.

The New Retirement Is…Active

Today's retirees are not content to stay home, working on the crossword puzzle. When possible, they travel the world, go on hikes and even run marathons. In fact, half of all men (and 40 percent of women) who finish marathons are competing in the "masters" category, meaning that they're over age 40. In 2016, Ed Whitlock ran the Toronto Waterfront Marathon in under four hours—at age 85.

One benefit of leaving the working world is that you'll now have more time to stay fit. Entering retirement or semiretirement correlates with an uptick in physical activity, according to a study of Americans ages 50 to 70 by scientists at the Early Start Research Institute. Keeping physically active as you get older is not just about looking (and feeling) good—it can also prolong your life. According to the National Institutes of Health, engaging in regular physical activity can increase life expectancies by more than four years.

The New Retirement Is… Geographically Mobile

Thanks to advancements in technology, it's now easier than ever to enjoy a mobile retirement while still being able to stay in touch with friends and family members—and even earning some extra income while you are on the road. While the changing public health situation has made travel difficult, it has also accelerated the trend toward remote-work arrangements, which ultimately give those who choose to work in retirement increased mobility. If there's a reliable Wi-Fi connection wherever you're headed, you're all set.

Many retirees make their home on the road, living part or full time in recreational vehicles. RV living is a way to travel while bringing the comforts of home along with you. RV ownership in America has been growing substantially over the last several years. And in response to the demand from today's active retirees, RV parks have even added yoga classes, bike rentals and running paths.

Moving abroad in retirement is also becoming an increasingly popular choice: The number of retirees who asked the Social Security Administration to mail their checks to an address in a foreign country increased by 50 percent between 2004 and 2014. Expat retirees are frequently drawn to places that offer a low cost of living and a temperate climate. The strength of the dollar against foreign currencies helps those on a fixed income get more bang for their buck. Meanwhile, video-chat services like Skype, Zoom and FaceTime make it easier than ever to stay connected to loved ones back home. ∎

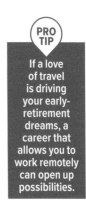

PRO TIP

If a love of travel is driving your early-retirement dreams, a career that allows you to work remotely can open up possibilities.

| 01 | FIND YOUR WHY | 01 | 02 | 03 | 04 | 05 | 06 | 07 |

Mission Critical
Understand Why You Want to Retire Early

It's easy to get stuck in a traditional view of careers and retirement: You toil away at the day-to-day, clocking your time until you can retire on Easy Street. Along the way, you put some money toward your retirement savings—and you treat yourself to little indulgences, like a big new TV or some retail therapy, to make it all a bit more bearable. But it doesn't have to be that way.

Instead, you can prioritize saving more now and make it to Easy Street that much sooner. Reaching this goal won't be easy. But as with any effort that requires hard work and sacrifice, the outcome is sure to be worthwhile.

One key to your success: Be very clear about exactly why you want to retire ahead of schedule. And this is one case where "I hate my job" won't cut it—the relief of stopping work will ebb quickly. Without more meaningful motivation to replace it, you may find yourself feeling dissatisfied and adrift. So consider whether the following reasons to pursue early retirement resonate with you—or can inspire you to dream up a purpose of your own.

Health

The phrase "Health is wealth" has never been more relevant. So you likely already understand that our health is our greatest asset, and full-time work—especially if you sit in a chair all day—can be counterproductive to remaining physically active. Retiring early gives you time to engage in activities that keep your mind sharp and your body strong, ensuring that the items on your bucket list are never out of reach due to health restrictions.

Relationships

Many retirees look forward to spending more time with their loved ones as they transition into the next phase,

PRO TIP

Once you've determined your "why," write it down and put it someplace you'll see each day to help you stay motivated and focused.

even if that means phone calls and video chats for now. Friends and family add meaning to life, and you shouldn't have to wait until you're 65 years old to make memories. Retiring early allows you to strengthen the relationships that bring you the most joy and—eventually—form new relationships with like-minded people who are pursuing shared interests and hobbies. You will also have more time to dedicate to older relatives who may need assistance in their later years, as well as give necessary attention to the younger generations, who will be looking to you as they develop their personal values.

More time for hobbies is a common motivator for early retirement.

Travel

As social restrictions ease, travel will reclaim its central place among many retirees' goals. Early retirement can help you see all of the world you want, as it allows you to travel without time constraints—or typical health limitations due to age. At the same time, advances in technology have created ample opportunities for part-time remote work, if you want to make money along the way. Relocating to a place with a lower cost of living or traveling through countries where the dollar goes a long way can help cut down on expenses and allow you to travel at your own pace.

Flexibility for Unforeseen Circumstances

Life throws curveballs—whether you're prepared or not. Pursuing a smart, strategic plan for early retirement can put you in a more stable financial position in the event that you need to rely on your savings earlier than expected. When a family member falls ill and needs a caretaker, when a sudden economic shock causes you to lose your job, when things you've taken for granted about the future prove uncertain, you're more prepared because you're already on an accelerated path to retirement. Account for uncertainty as you prepare for your retirement years. Remember to talk with loved ones about how unforeseen circumstances may modify your approach.

Because of the changes in technology, medical care and societal expectations of this phase of life, retirement can start significantly earlier for those who define their goals, stay focused and work hard to meet them. The decisions you make now will greatly affect your time line for transitioning into retirement—so remember the "why," and your answers will help you make your goal a reality. ∎

01   **THREE STAGES**   01 | 02 | 03 | 04 | 05 | 06 | 07

The Three-Stage Retirement
How It Affects Your Finances

In your working years, it's easy to look at retirement as a single, glorious phase full of freedom, leisure and fulfillment. If you're planning on retiring early, however, it's useful to take a more nuanced approach, seeing as you may live 30 or 40 years—or more—in retirement. After all, retired life in your late 80s might bear little resemblance to retired life in your 50s—and calls for a very different financial strategy.

To ensure that your financial plan meets your needs at all points, view retirement as progressing through three broad stages.

STAGE 1
The Active Early Years

Many new retirees—and especially those who've managed to quit the daily grind ahead of schedule—seize the chance to travel, socialize and cultivate long-held interests. Far from sedentary, the first stage of retirement can be more active and energizing than your working years.

With a newly open schedule, now is the time to try a new hobby, rekindle old friendships or take that exotic vacation you've always dreamed of. During this stage, you may also wish to continue working, perhaps on a part-time schedule or giving back to your profession in a mentor capacity.

With its potential adventure, this first stage of retirement can be a time when expenses run high. You'll need to budget for increased travel and other discretionary spending while taking care not to blow through too much of your savings. On the investing front, many assume retirement means moving assets into a thoroughly conservative portfolio. But that's usually not the case in your first years—especially if you've retired young. You'll want to keep a portion of funds invested in stocks so that they can continue to grow and help fund your later retirement stages.

PRO TIP

If heavy travel is in your plans, you may want to budget to do the bulk of your traveling in the early, healthiest years of retirement.

Your financial planning may shift throughout your retirement years.

The Calmer Middle Years

Usually between ages 70 and 80, your lifestyle is prone to start slowing down. That doesn't mean you stop cultivating the hobbies and interests that animated the first stage of your retirement; you might just fit more relaxation in between to recharge. Retirees at this stage tend to keep closer to home and spend more time with friends and family. While staying relatively active, they also allow retired life to settle into a pleasant sense of routine that might resemble traditional retirement more than the go-go-go early years did.

This stage often has the lowest regular expenses, even as medical costs tend to increase. You're less likely to spend as much money on trips and activities and may no longer need to be supporting other family members financially.

17

The early years of retirement are often active and fulfilling.

You may also sell your house and downsize to a smaller living space or move to a less expensive location. Many retirees will lean toward more conservative investment portfolios during this stage while still keeping some of their savings in stocks.

STAGE 3

The Winding-Down Years

From about age 80 onward, retirees tend to spend more and more time at home. Travel and other activities decrease as one's energy wanes, but it's never more important to tend to your well-being, often through time spent with those closest to you. Younger family members are often a crucial source of support in this life stage.

Increased medical and long-term-care needs drive up a person's costs in these later years, but that rise in expenses is often countered by reduced spending on travel and outdoor activities. While your regular budget will likely be pared down to the essentials, the winding-down stage may also be a time when you focus on passing down assets to the next generation or on securing a philanthropic legacy.

Viewing your future retirement in phases gives you a framework to build a more detailed and secure financial strategy. When you have a strong plan in place, along with a willingness to modify it as circumstances change, you're in a better position to make the most of your early retirement years while not shortchanging the later ones. ■

Keys to Retirement Success #1
Preparing Financially for a Long Retirement

Retirement planning tends to focus on money, and for good reason: Without a steady paycheck, you've got to be sure you have the cash you need to cover your expenses for the rest of your life. But it's also important to consider the other major contributors to a successful retirement: social connections and health. This section, and the two that follow, provide some ideas for how to think about each of these three critical factors.

The good news is we're living longer. A little more than 100 years ago, in 1900, the life expectancy for men in the U.S. was just 46.3 years, while women could expect to live to the not-so-ripe average age of 48.3, according to data from the Centers for Disease Control and Prevention (CDC). But thanks to advances in vaccines and antibiotics, as well as access to clean water, life expectancy has climbed dramatically in the past century. An American born in 2017 can expect to enjoy an average life span of 78.6 years, according to recent CDC statistics—a whopping

A longer life means you may need to accumulate more assets to support yourself.

30-plus years more than our forebears of the early 20th century.

While longevity means you'll likely have more years to enjoy your retirement, it also means you'll need to carefully craft a plan to make your money last—especially as an early retiree.

Longevity Risk

Living longer means most of us will have more time to live, love, play, work and learn. It's a very appealing prospect, and it shouldn't be underestimated. However, longevity also brings about several new challenges. Chief among them is adapting our financial planning efforts to support our lengthening lives. In fact, the Stanford Center on Longevity says underestimating life expectancy, and therefore the number of years we'll spend in retirement, is a common pitfall in retirement planning.

Longevity risk—the risk of outliving your money—is something every investor needs to consider. But as someone planning to retire early, you'll have a shorter time horizon to earn that money before you retire and a longer period of time in which you'll need your assets to support you. Because you'll need to fund 30, 40 or more years of postretirement life, you'll need to plan aggressively and creatively in order to reach your goal. You'll also need to realistically forecast your future expenses, such as housing, health care and discretionary spending.

PRO TIP
Your best bet for fighting longevity risk: Plan well, save carefully and slash your expenses aggressively during your working years.

What Longevity Means for Early Retirees

To reach your goal of early retirement in an age of longevity, you'll need to brainstorm ways to ramp up your savings by finding new sources of income, such as a side hustle or real estate investment. You'll also want to look at slashing your expenses, which could include downsizing your home or minimizing transportation costs.

As you plan for early retirement, there will be other issues to consider, including where you'll live—both in terms of your home size and your geographical location—once you retire.

Last but not least, health care and health insurance are among the biggest financial obstacles currently facing early retirees. A study by the Society of Actuaries found that 67 percent of preretirees were concerned about health care costs in retirement—a logical worry, considering there may be a few decades before you're eligible for Medicare, and the future of the Affordable Care Act is uncertain. Options for dealing with health insurance include medical tourism, health care ministries, moving to a country with universal health care or continuing to work part time for health care benefits.

Early retirement during an era of longer life spans can be a challenge, but with some flexibility and forethought—and the helpful hints that you'll find in the following pages—you can reach your goals. ∎

> More years spent living an active, healthy life is a blessing—but it also means taking careful steps to ensure all of your needs are fully met.

Your retirement could last 30 to 40 years or more.

Keys to Retirement Success #2
The Importance of Social Connections

It's no secret: Having a strong social network contributes to our overall happiness and provides benefits for both our physical and mental well-being. To enjoy a satisfying, full life as an early retiree, you'll need to spend some time considering what your social life will look like in retirement. This is particularly important because social isolation was on the rise even before masks and social distancing became a way of life thanks to the global pandemic. An AARP study recently determined that more than a third of Americans ages 45 and up reported experiencing loneliness.

As we're all learning firsthand, the impact of social isolation on our well-being is significant. Connect2Affect, an AARP-backed project, claims that sustained social isolation presents the same health risks as one might experience smoking 15 cigarettes a day. Research at the Rush Alzheimer's Disease Center in Chicago indicates that loneliness is also linked to an increased risk for dementia.

The Social Challenges of Early Retirement

Most of us find that it gets trickier to make new friends as we age. While social circles used to be forged on the playground, in student clubs or in dorm rooms, as we settle into the adult routines of work and family, cultivating new friendships isn't always as easy.

For many of us, our social life is tied strongly to our workplace. An HP workplace survey found that 56 percent of workers spend more time with their colleagues than their family. What's more, the act of retiring tends to shrink our social network, according to a study by the Center for Retirement Research at Boston College that came to the same conclusion.

Even under normal circumstances, as someone planning for early retirement, you can expect that creating and maintaining strong social connections may pose a challenge. When you've achieved your goal of being able to shape your days as you see fit, many—if not most—of your buddies will still be toiling away on the weekdays. And if travel, relocation or nomadic living is part of your vision for early retirement, that brings additional challenges.

Making a Plan for Your Future Social Life

The good news is that just as you're creating a financial road map for early retirement, you can start making changes now to boost your likelihood of a well-connected life in retirement.

Start by contemplating your interests. Are you a dedicated yogi or a mountain-biking fanatic? Is there a social cause you're passionate about or an artistic pursuit you've always wanted to try but haven't? Think about how you might want to spend your early retirement in a post-pandemic world, then start finding ways to engage in those activities in a community setting. Volunteering, taking a class or getting involved in civic activities, clubs or church groups that interest you are all easy ways to begin widening your social circle.

Until then, the internet offers an easy way to find and connect with like-minded people. If you haven't already, check out some of the online communities dedicated to early retirement, such as Mr. Money Mustache, early-retirement. org or Early Retirement Extreme. Becoming part of an online early-retirement community can broaden your social network—and also allows you to swap tips and ideas.

Also remember that your diverse interests—hobbies, career background, volunteer work—provide natural ways to make connections with like-minded people. As an early retiree, you may find your new social circle includes a wider array of people than you interacted with in your working days—people who are older or younger but with whom you share common ground. Being open to new possibilities can help you forge and maintain relationships. ∎

Socializing isn't just pleasurable—it's also good for your health.

Keys to Retirement Success #3
Healthy Practices to Support Decades of Retirement

You've established why you want to retire early, whether you want more time for creative pursuits or travel or you're tired of the corporate world.

To get the most out of your life in early retirement and beyond, you'll want to be in optimal health—both physically and mentally. Below are some of the top practices correlated with longevity.

Exercise, Exercise, Exercise

Getting regular exercise has been shown to increase longevity and lower stress. A fitness routine doesn't have to mean hitting the gym. The best way to stay consistent is to figure out what type of exercise you enjoy, whether it's dancing, swimming, walking or team sports.

It's never too late to start enjoying the benefits of regular exercise. A study published in the *British Journal of Sports Medicine* showed that elderly men who participated in 30 minutes of physical activity six days a week lived about five years longer than their inactive peers.

Develop Healthy Eating Habits

A 2016 Harvard study showed that people who ate a diet rich in plant-based proteins had lower mortality risk than those who relied more heavily on animal-based proteins. In particular, those who ate a diet high in red meat had an increased risk of death from cardiovascular and other diseases. A plant-based diet may not only help you live longer, it also could allow you to save more money, since plant-based proteins such as beans and soy are more affordable than meat. And it doesn't have to be all or nothing: You can gain health benefits with even small tweaks in your eating habits.

PRO TIP

Connecting with others interested in early retirement can help you make like-minded friends and keep you motivated.

Use some of your new spare time to keep up with friends old and new.

Manage Your Stress

We all experience stress, but how we deal with it could make a huge difference in how we age. Meditation is one popular, research-backed way to reduce stress levels, change the way our cells age and possibly extend our life span. Studies have found that meditation promotes activity of the enzyme telomerase in the brain, which can help fight cellular aging.

And you don't have to sit cross-legged for hours on end to reap the benefits of meditation. Even meditating for 10 minutes can provide physical and mental benefits. Need help getting started? Meditation apps make it easier than ever to incorporate a meditation practice into our lives.

Find Your Tribe

As previously mentioned, maintaining strong social connections is crucial to our health and longevity. An almost 80-year-long Harvard study that followed men throughout their lifetimes showed a major correlation between the men's relationships and their health and happiness. Participants who were highly satisfied with their relationships in their 50s were healthier at age 80. ■

Retirement Savings
Your Magic Number

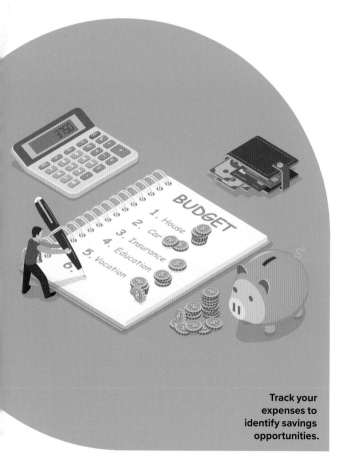

Track your expenses to identify savings opportunities.

With people living longer and receiving fewer retirement benefits from employers, the importance of saving for your golden years is pretty clear. And if you're planning to retire early, it's even more crucial. But knowing just how much you need to put away in order to live comfortably—your magic number—is more complicated. Conventional wisdom suggests saving a fixed percentage of your annual income, and some experts even advocate saving a standard dollar amount. While those strategies can be a good starting point, the formulas only go so far. Rather than an arbitrary goal, consider targeting a more tangible number—your anticipated expenses.

By projecting the cost of both necessary living expenses and lifestyle goals during retirement, you can make a far more accurate estimate of how much money you'll need to meet them. This estimate can help you develop a personalized savings strategy to help ensure you have the money to pay for what you need and care about most.

Check your projected retirement budget against your savings to see how close you are to your goal.

Creating a Budget

Comparing your projected needs in retirement with your current savings allows you to identify potential shortfalls and ultimately set a savings goal to work toward. Begin by tracking the essential and discretionary costs you currently have, including monthly expenses like food, housing and transportation as well as items like property taxes, auto registrations and any insurance policies that are paid on a yearly basis. Also consider your spending on hobbies and entertainment. These figures will give you a sense of what it will cost to maintain your lifestyle once you've left work. Estimate the costs of your discretionary goals, such as travel or buying a vacation home, and add those to your budget as well.

Keep in mind that while some costs will decrease as you enter retirement, others will grow. For example, if you're planning on paying down your mortgage or downsizing before retirement, your housing costs, including property taxes and utilities, could be considerably less than what they are now. Health care, however, may become more expensive. According to an annual study by Fidelity Investments, couples can expect to pay, on average, $275,000 in out-of-pocket medical costs over the course of their retirement. If you retire before qualifying for Medicare at age 65, the costs could be higher. Without access to coverage through your employer, you'll be responsible for bridging that health insurance gap yourself.

Remember, retirement can last for decades. Consider that a quarter of 65-year-olds will live to be at least 90, according to the Social Security Administration. If you're retiring

PRO TIP

Downsizing your home and cutting back on housing expenses can help you add to your savings during your retirement years.

When planning for your financial needs, it pays to err on the side of being overcautious.

early, your money will need to last even longer. When planning for your financial needs, it's better to account for more time than it is to risk outliving your money.

Tightening Your Belt

With fewer years to accumulate savings, early retirees have to take a more aggressive savings approach. And if your current savings strategy is still too conservative to meet your projected retirement savings goal, trimming your living costs is the best way to free up cash so you can retire on time.

Start by targeting discretionary items—try ditching an expensive cable package for a low-cost streaming service or making more meals at home instead of eating at restaurants multiple times each week. Making those smaller changes now can pay big dividends over time. But in order to add significantly to your savings, forgoing your daily latte isn't going to be enough. Ask yourself if downsizing your home could be an option, or if you can refinance your mortgage at a lower rate. If your household owns multiple vehicles, maybe you could manage with just one. Cutting expenses can also help make the transition to retirement a smoother one, allowing you to ease into a more sustainable lifestyle.

With focus and discipline, you can reach your own magic number and retire according to the schedule you've set. ∎

In the later stages of retirement, family is often a top priority.

Location Is Everything

From the expat lifestyle to retirement-friendly
U.S. towns, a look at your many options

Downsizing vs. Staying Put
Should You Stay or Go?

For many retirees and preretirees, moving into a smaller house can be a natural and positive step in downsizing your lifestyle. The kids are gone, leaving behind empty bedrooms and boxes of unneeded stuff. And many of us start to ask ourselves, "What's the point of paying for all that space if much of it is collecting dust?"

Indeed, there are good reasons to consider downsizing as retirement approaches, including the fact that it provides a chance to simplify and declutter your life. If you move into a smaller house, you'll have less space, so moving provides an excellent opportunity to decide what's really worth hanging on to. You may find that you don't actually need (or have a strong attachment to) a surprising proportion of your possessions—including furniture, appliances, clothes, books and items belonging to your adult children. You may also find you can do with one car rather than two or more, and getting rid of a vehicle could bring significant annual savings—plus, it's one less thing to worry about.

With careful planning, downsizing can make life more manageable while saving you extra money. Those savings can help make this approach part of a comprehensive plan that allows for an early or partial retirement. But before you make the leap, it's important to consider the following ramifications.

Housing Costs

The prospect of paying less for housing is often a primary motive for downsizing. Trading a $500,000 five-bedroom home for a $300,000 two-bedroom home frees up a lot of money for everyday expenses, travel and other costs. If you invest some or all of that money, you'll see even greater profits in the long run. What's more, couples who have used a home as their primary residence for at least two of the past five years can exclude up

PRO TIP

When making a long-distance move, it may make more sense to rent a place to live before buying to help you find the best fit for your needs.

Do you envision a beach lifestyle, or do you prefer the mountains?

to $500,000 in capital gains from any income gained from selling their home. (Single filers can exclude up to $250,000.) Because this gain is tax-free, more of the income you generate from downsizing can be used right away. Remember that not all gain will be profit; you may have to pay a real estate agent up to a 6 percent commission.

Moving Costs

Moving can be expensive. Hiring a moving company can be a significant expense, especially if you're moving to a distant state or to another country. For example, the average moving company cost for a move from Florida to California or vice versa was $4,047, according to data collected

33

Before you settle in at your dream locale, it may make sense to rent for a few months.

by My Moving Reviews. You may also face other, smaller costs that can add up. For example, you might face charges from utility companies to open or close accounts, and you'll almost certainly need to buy at least a few new things to set up your new place. Your own travel costs can add up as well. Be sure to factor in all these expenses when determining the cost of a move.

Taxes

Depending on where you live now and where you're considering living, state-tax differences could provide a major incentive (or disincentive) to relocate. For example, if you move to a smaller, less-expensive home in a state with higher property taxes, your savings will be less dramatic than they would be if you stayed in state.

Consider all state and local taxes, including income, sales, property and estate taxes, before moving. Some states, like Florida and Texas, don't have an income tax. Others, like Oregon and Montana, don't have a sales tax. Still other states offer senior-specific tax breaks that will come in handy, or exempt Social Security benefits and other forms of retirement income from their income taxes. (For more on important tax considerations, see "Calculating Taxes Into Your Decision to Move" on page 36.)

Cost of Living

Everyday expenses, like groceries and transportation, can vary widely from place to place, and even slightly higher costs can add up over the long run. Downsizing often leads to lower utility bills, but this is not always the case. For example, if you're moving to a place with a hotter climate, you may end up paying more for air conditioning. The cost of health insurance and car insurance is another important factor to consider.

Lifestyle

Downsizing offers an opportunity to move to a place that better suits your lifestyle. Many people want greater access to the outdoors, whether that means the ocean, mountains or a state or national park. Others put a premium on access to cultural resources such as live music, museums and restaurants. When considering whether to move to a new place, be sure to weigh these considerations against other lifestyle factors, such as weather and proximity to friends and family. You might think you want to live at the beach, but if it means putting up with triple-digit temperatures for several months of the year and seeing your family less, you may want to ask: Is the beach lifestyle really worth it?

The Option to Rent

While many homeowners are reluctant to give up the satisfaction of owning their own place, there may be substantial benefits to renting rather than buying—especially when making a big move. After all, renting is less of a risk than buying, and it allows you to change your mind more easily if your new location doesn't work out. Consult your financial adviser to discuss whether renting might make sense for your circumstances.

Staying put in retirement offers plenty of advantages, not the least of which is avoiding the stress and upheaval that comes with moving somewhere else. Remaining in a comfortable and stimulating social circle can also be a strong enticement to stay. If you want to downsize, do your research first to give yourself the best chance at sticking your landing. ■

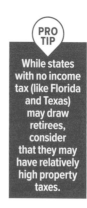

PRO TIP

While states with no income tax (like Florida and Texas) may draw retirees, consider that they may have relatively high property taxes.

Calculating Taxes Into Your Decision to Move
Choosing the Right Location to Avoid Taxation

If you're considering making the move to retire early, it's important to get an accurate analysis of the true cost of living in your desired location, which includes the cost of both state and local taxes. As an early retiree, you will have had less time to save than your older peers, and therefore will need your savings to last for a longer amount of time. That's why paying particular attention to tax efficiencies is of critical importance.

Taxes vary widely by both state and locale. For example, Washington State does not have a broad-based income tax, which means retirees don't have to pay income taxes on their Social Security benefits, pensions or other retirement income. However, combined state and local sales tax rates there are some of the highest in the nation—up to 10.5 percent—and property taxes are steep.

When deciding whether to move or stay put, take a close look at these five types of taxes.

State Income Tax

Stay up to date on income-tax rates and how they'll affect different forms of retirement income, such as Social Security, retirement accounts and other investments. Nine states—Alaska, Florida, Nevada, New Hampshire, South Dakota, Texas, Tennessee, Washington State and Wyoming—do not have individual income tax. Of the states that do levy income tax, the number of brackets varies: For example, Alabama has a three-bracket income-tax system, ranging from 2 to 5 percent; California has 10 brackets that range from 1.1 to 14.63 percent.

Local Tax

Some states allow cities, counties and municipalities to levy local income taxes. While some are permanent, others are

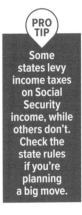

PRO TIP

Some states levy income taxes on Social Security income, while others don't. Check the state rules if you're planning a big move.

House-hunting can be fun, but don't forget to factor in property taxes.

temporary and fund specific projects for education, parks and community improvements. Each state has different local tax rules—from flat rates to income-based rates that may exempt some retirees, depending on their fixed income. If you're planning to relocate to the District of Columbia or one of these 17 states—Alabama, Arkansas, California, Colorado, Delaware, Indiana, Iowa, Kansas, Kentucky, Maryland, Michigan, Missouri, New Jersey, New York, Ohio, Oregon or Pennsylvania—make sure to look into local taxes before you go.

Social Security Tax

Social Security benefits are a guaranteed form of income that can help you cover your recurring and variable expenses. Thirteen states—Colorado, Connecticut, Kansas, Minnesota, Missouri, Montana, Nebraska, New Mexico, North Dakota, Rhode Island, Utah, Vermont and West Virginia—apply taxes to Social Security. If you move to one of these states, plan on having some of your Social Security income go to taxes, which will reduce your monthly check. That said, if your only source of retirement income is from Social Security, some states will offer an exemption.

Property Tax

If you're planning to buy a home in another state, evaluate property taxes closely. Many states that don't have income taxes make up for it with high property taxes that can hit people on fixed incomes hard. Some states will offer property-tax-relief programs for older individuals or those with limited income or disabilities. Every program has different qualifiers, so assess each one carefully. If you're set on moving to a high-property-tax state, consider whether renting may be a cheaper alternative to owning and paying taxes.

Consider state rules on inheritance tax as you plan for the future.

Inheritance Tax

It never hurts to plan for the future, so consider state rules on inheritance tax. Currently, only six states collect inheritance tax—Iowa, Kentucky, Maryland, Nebraska, New Jersey and Pennsylvania. If you live in one of these states, your beneficiaries may have to pay taxes on the assets you pass down to them, though the threshold at which those taxes kick in varies wildly. Fortunately, spouses are tax-exempt when it comes to inheriting property, and only Nebraska and Pennsylvania collect inheritance taxes on property passing to children and grandchildren.

Understanding state and local taxes can help you anticipate what will work for you financially in the decades to come. Whether you decide to move to a new state or to continue enjoying the opportunities in your current location, it's always beneficial to know your options.

One last piece of advice: If you decide to relocate, make sure you clearly establish residency in your new state: Obtain a driver's license or state-issued ID, change your address on important documents, register to vote, open an account with a local bank, register your car, buy or rent property and file a resident income tax return. These steps will help your case should your former state try to collect taxes after you've moved. ∎

PRO TIP

Consider estate and inheritance taxes if you're hoping to leave a significant amount in assets to your loved ones after you die.

Your family's financial health may also be a consideration in your retirement planning.

Some early retirees favor an exotic location with a low cost of living.

The Ins and Outs of Retiring Abroad
Is the Expat Lifestyle Right for You?

There are many reasons that retiring overseas is appealing at any age: the weather, the natural beauty, the opportunities for adventure. But with so many retirement accounts taking a hit in the recession, the lower cost of living in many foreign countries has become even more appealing. And the severity of potential health issues underscores a crucial criterion for an overseas retirement destination: access to great medical care. Malaysia, for example, was already a popular choice for U.S. expats looking to stretch their dollars in a tropical, English-friendly country. But its lauded health care system may be the thing that keeps U.S. retirees relocating there.

Consider Cost of Living

Many retirees gravitate to countries with lower costs of living in order to stretch their savings further. Spending less on things like food, bills and transportation can enable you to enjoy a higher standard of living than you would back home—or make your money last longer in your new favorite place. *The Economist*'s Worldwide Cost of Living survey, which is easily found online, can help you determine how a potential new home measures up. For a more detailed budget breakdown, consult websites catering to expats in the country of your choice. These sources can help you get a sense of how much your peers are spending on things like rent, travel and health care.

Before you start daydreaming about moving into an oceanfront villa, consider that some major expenses might be the same—or even larger—abroad. If you opt to live in a major tourist area, for example, you may find that rents and restaurants are pricey. You'll likely pay a premium for foods and other products imported from the U.S. Currency-conversion fees may erode your savings. And if you plan on making regular

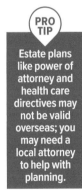

PRO TIP

Estate plans like power of attorney and health care directives may not be valid overseas; you may need a local attorney to help with planning.

visits to see friends and family who still live in the U.S., it's important to also factor in a hefty travel budget to cover the cost of airfare.

Understand Visa and Other Requirements

Every country has different visa requirements and rules about residency. Consult the U.S. State Department's website for specific information about your country of choice to ensure your relocation meets all the legal requirements.

If your retirement plans include working or purchasing property abroad, make sure those options are available to you in your new home. Local employment laws may limit the kind or amount of work that can be done by foreign workers. Buying property overseas can be a tricky prospect; as a foreigner, you may not be eligible for a mortgage. Some countries restrict foreigners' ability to own property or require permits and government permission before you can do so. If you can't buy a property, renting may be your best option.

Make a Health Care Plan

Many seniors rely on Medicare to cover health care costs in retirement. But retirees living abroad have to make alternate plans, as the program typically doesn't cover overseas medical care. And of course, retired people who aren't yet eligible for Medicare must do the same.

PRO TIP

As long as you're a U.S. citizen, you'll unfortunately still have to file a tax return, even if you're living in another country full time.

That leaves expats with a few options. They can purchase supplemental insurance that will cover them in their new home; they can maintain a U.S. health plan and return to the U.S. for medical care;

or, if they relocate to a country with a nationalized health care system and are eligible for treatment, they can get care that way. Be sure to thoroughly research the benefits and risks of the options in your new country before dropping coverage in the U.S.

Whatever option you choose, you may also want to buy medical evacuation insurance to cover the significant cost of an emergency evacuation. Chances are, you'll never need it—but you'll be very glad to have it if you do.

Know Your Tax Liabilities

Even if you're living outside the country full time and plan to do so permanently, you still have to file a U.S. tax return if you're a U.S. citizen or resident alien. According to federal law, Americans living abroad have the same obligation to file income-, estate- and gift-tax returns, just as they would if they were still living domestically.

When it comes to state tax, the process is more complicated. Every state has different residency criteria, although in many cases, you can end your residency if you can prove you live outside the state for more than six months a year. If you're still earning money in your previous home state—for example, you lease your house and accrue rental income—you may owe state taxes on that income, if it exceeds a certain threshold.

In addition to federal income tax, you may be subject to taxes in your new country as well. The good news is that U.S. citizens who retire abroad can benefit from tax credits and deductions that may reduce their overall tax bill. The Foreign Earned Income Exclusion allows you to exclude a portion of the income you've earned in a foreign country from your taxes; you may also be able to take either a tax credit or a deduction for the amount you pay in foreign taxes on that income. ∎

It's critical to understand your health care options when retiring abroad.

Get a Head Start on Seeing the World
Become a Digital Nomad

If long-term social distancing has got you more determined than ever to see the world as travel finally opens back up, you may want to consider joining the ranks of digital nomads. Digital nomads are people in all stages of their careers who take their laptops and set off for beautiful places. Some work only as much as needed to get by, while others save money for the future by reducing their cost of living.

Many are independent contractors, but others work for startups or global corporations. More employers are seeing the wisdom in letting their employees choose where to work.

If you're interested in becoming a digital nomad, you'll want to think carefully about how to make it work for your unique situation.

What to Do for Work
Any job that requires nothing more than a laptop and an internet connection can be done remotely.

Some of the more common digital-nomad jobs include graphic design, coding, IT consulting and software development. Of course, if you want to work for your current employer, you'll need to get permission to ditch the office, if you haven't done so already. And you'll need to establish clear expectations with your manager and colleagues about when you'll be available and how you'll stay in touch. This clarity will go a long way in making this new phase of your career successful.

If you work for yourself as an entrepreneur or an independent contractor, you may find it easier to transition to life as a digital nomad than your office-bound counterparts. Writers and other creative freelancers can find online work through sites like Upwork and Fiverr—though getting gigs isn't always easy, especially for less-experienced freelancers. (And, of course,

PRO TIP

Make sure you have enough time for fun: Consider relocating to an area with a nice climate and a low cost of living so your money goes further.

Got wanderlust? The digital-nomad lifestyle means that you can work on the road.

45

For travel-hungry retirees, collecting passport stamps can be a favorite pastime.

those sites take a cut of the fee.) Whether you work for yourself or someone else, it's a good idea to test out the remote lifestyle by doing at least a few months of work from your current home.

Where to Go

Part of the appeal of working remotely is the freedom to live where you want. Digital nomads typically seek out places that are beautiful and cheap, with temperate climates. Lisbon, Madrid, Cape Town, Bali and northern Thailand have long been popular choices. As travelers become more conscious of the importance of maintaining access to a great health care system, their preferences may change. Some remote workers hop from place to place, based on how much they expect to bring in during certain parts of the year. Others do the same out of nothing more than a thirst for new experiences.

Climate, cost and community can all factor in to where you go.

community, and this aspect shouldn't be overlooked if you decide to work in far-flung places.

A New Option for Digital Nomads

The past few years have seen the emergence of a new kind of company that caters to the digital-nomad community. For a fee, these companies find or supply housing for remote workers—and, in some cases, coordinate travel and introduce fellow workers to one another.

WiFi Tribe, for example, provides shared or private rooms in Florence, Italy; Quito, Ecuador; Taghazout, Morocco and other places for a monthly membership of between $800 and $1,800. Nomad House and Unsettled offer 30-day stays at houses and apartments they lease around the world. Another company, Roam, maintains permanent co-living spaces in Miami, London, Tokyo and Bali. These companies typically provide places to relax and interact, as well as work space and communal kitchens.

While climate, cost of living and access to health care are important factors, just as important is the social experience you'll have as a digital nomad. Certain cities, such as Canggu, Bali, or Chiang Mai, Thailand, are popular destinations because you can typically count on finding other people there who speak your language and have chosen a similar lifestyle. The traditional office space, for all its drawbacks, fosters human interaction and a sense of

If you choose to become a digital nomad, you don't want to find yourself stuck in a foreign country. Make sure you set aside money for an emergency fund and get good travel insurance. It's also a good idea to minimize debt before you head off for parts unknown. And if the nomad life isn't for you? The office is likely to still be there when you get home. ∎

PRO TIP

Portable careers include information technology, coding, consulting, graphic design, software development and creative professions.

10 U.S. Hot Spots for Active Retirees
Find Walking Trails, Restaurants, Museums and More in These Communities

Bend has plenty to offer in the way of outdoor recreation.

Retiring doesn't have to mean slowing down: Staying engaged can be simply a matter of living in an engaging community. If you want to be where things are happening, consider a retirement destination that will help you pursue your interests, whether that's exploring the outdoors, attending lectures or working a part-time job. Here are 10 places in the U.S. where you can enjoy an active retirement.

Bend, Oregon
Despite Oregon's reputation for rain, Bend gets less than a foot per year, thanks to its high elevation. The dry climate and proximity to the Deschutes River and Cascade Mountain Range make it a go-to for outdoor recreation. Residents fish, bike and kayak through the summer season. In winter, nearby Mount Bachelor ski resort offers skiing, snowboarding and snowshoeing. For culture, check out Bend's Munch & Music concert series each summer, as well as productions by the acclaimed Cascades Theatrical Company.

Broomfield, Colorado

Broomfield is ideal for nature lovers, featuring some 250 miles of trails, with Chautauqua Park, Eldorado Canyon State Park and Rocky Mountain National Park just a 90-minute drive away. Active retirees may also enjoy Broomfield Days in September, with a parade and 5K race. It's not hard for retirees to make friends here: About a third of the population is age 50 or over.

Chattanooga, Tennessee

Enjoy Chattanooga's beautiful scenery and walkability. From downtown, locals can jog or bike along the Tennessee Riverwalk, a scenic trail that extends 13 miles to Chickamauga Dam. The town offers riverfront townhouse and condo options, thanks to a $120 million development project completed in the past decade. Despite high sales tax, Tennessee doesn't tax income and is phasing out dividend taxes.

Galveston, Texas

Healthy tourist traffic has made Galveston a vibrant coastal community for all ages. Foodies flock to the island's annual Food and Wine Festival, while concertgoers enjoy summer shows at Moody Gardens. Lifelong learners can check out programming and lectures at Galveston College and Texas A&M's Galveston branch. Galveston offers an affordable seaside lifestyle because of its relatively cheap real estate and Texas' lack of income tax. And Houston is a quick 45-minute drive north.

Hoboken is close to Manhattan—but without the cost.

Hoboken, New Jersey

Hoboken is all about "location, location, location." This highly walkable New York neighbor sits just across the Hudson River to the west of Manhattan and gives residents stellar views of—and access to—New York City, at lower prices than they would find in the Big Apple. Grab a quick PATH train or ferry ride into Manhattan for boundless dining, shopping and entertainment options. And Hoboken also has plenty of cultural goings-on of its own, including top-notch restaurants, art galleries and outdoor activities, like movie screenings and festivals in the summer, as well as parks, walking paths and community services.

Lincoln has a small-town feel with a sophisticated edge.

restaurants. Residents can head to nearby Marco Island for picturesque party-boating and exploring. And to the northeast lies Corkscrew Swamp Sanctuary, where an elevated boardwalk rewards visitors with fascinating views of wetland birds, gators and other wildlife.

Northfield, Minnesota

This college town is ideal for lifetime learners. Northfield is home to St. Olaf College and Carleton College, both of which offer frequent lectures, movie screenings and theater performances. The Cannon Valley Elder Collegium holds liberal arts courses for older students. Outdoorsy types will enjoy canoeing or kayaking the Cannon River in summer and snowshoeing Cowling Arboretum, near Carleton, in winter.

Lincoln, Nebraska

Avid runners and bikers will enjoy this heartland city's network of more than 130 miles of trails, not to mention more than 6,000 acres of parks. Residents can enjoy a public market and various live entertainment options in the city's new Railyard entertainment district, as well as all the cultural offerings of this college town. But retirees should also take into account Nebraska's inheritance tax, which can reach 18 percent for funds not passed to a spouse or charity.

Portland, Maine

Maine's largest city boasts culture and nature. Coastal hikes and kayak outings are as easy to find as the lively restaurants and concerts. Merrill Auditorium is a go-to for classical performances, while Portland Stage puts on first-rate theater productions. For postcard-worthy views, nearby Mackworth Island and Peaks Island are hard to beat.

Naples, Florida

Naples offers a gorgeous coastline and serene sunsets over the Gulf of Mexico, but don't think that retired life here is sedentary. The lively downtown offers upscale art galleries and scenic outdoor

Santa Barbara, California

The perfectly mild climate means residents can hike, bike and surf year-round or enjoy the bevy of local parks and beaches for swimming and fishing. A trail system links the city's residential and shopping areas, facilitating a healthy daily routine for exercise enthusiasts. ∎

There's no shortage of sunshine or ways to enjoy it in Santa Barbara.

Housing & Transportation

Get a handle on your biggest expenses
to meet your early-retirement goals

03 **HOUSING COSTS** 01 | 02 | **03**

Controlling Housing Costs in Retirement
Options to Help Lower Your Living Expenses

Since retiring early means you'll have fewer years to accumulate savings, the key to meeting your goal—and making your money last throughout your lifetime—is reducing living expenses. And while making an effort to reduce costs like food and entertainment is helpful, the most important expense to target is housing.

Why? According to the Bureau of Labor Statistics, housing costs—which include mortgages, property taxes, insurance and maintenance—account for 31 percent of annual spending for those who are between the ages of 55 and 64. And those costs only become a larger part of the budget as you age: For retirees 65 and older, roughly 34 percent of an annual budget goes toward housing. In fact, someone who retires at age 55 will pay more than $355,000, on average, for housing during the first 20 years of retirement alone.

That makes managing—and, where possible, minimizing—those costs central to generating more savings and retiring on your own terms. Here are a number of different strategies for controlling your housing costs as you plan for—and enter—early retirement.

Pay Off Your Mortgage

Paying off your mortgage early means eliminating what is likely your largest monthly bill and saving on interest payments. It's a move that can improve cash flow and help you build a more comfortable savings cushion in case you experience an emergency.

However, paying down a home loan before you enter retirement isn't always easy or necessarily possible for everyone—even at a more traditional retirement age. In fact, roughly a third of homeowners between the ages of 65 and 74 are still carrying an average

PRO TIP

Paying off your mortgage ahead of schedule— or even refinancing your loan—can help position you financially for early retirement.

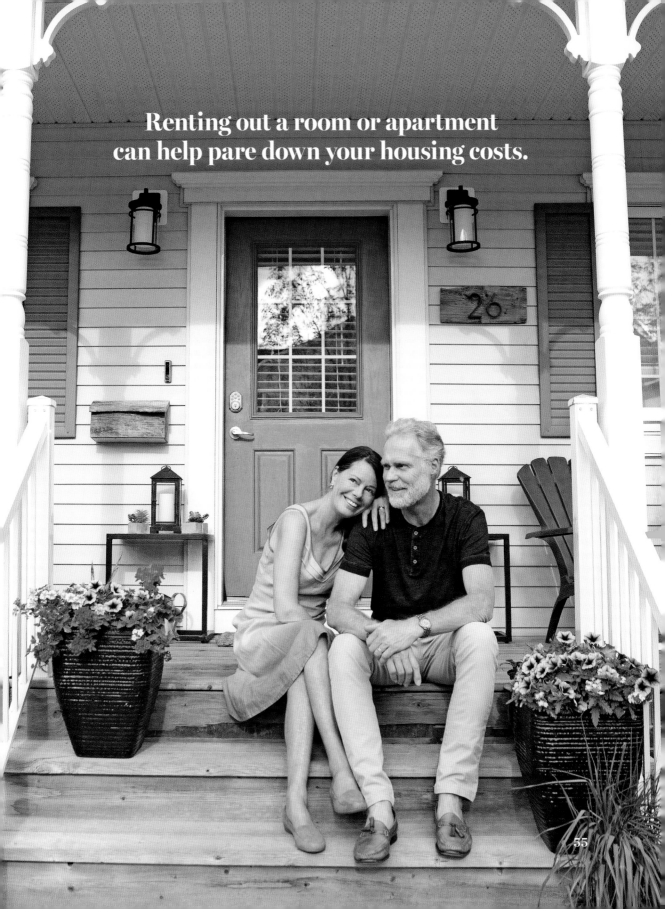

Renting out a room or apartment can help pare down your housing costs.

balance of $118,000 on their mortgage, according to the Federal Reserve. There may also be penalties for early payment.

If you're already putting extra money in savings so you can retire early, paying down significant mortgage debt years ahead of schedule can be more challenging. If you don't have extra cash to pay off your mortgage early, consider refinancing. Doing so won't eliminate your debt, but it may secure a lower interest rate, which can make your monthly mortgage payments more affordable.

Downsize

Moving into a smaller home can have a number of cost-saving benefits. Downsizing can help reduce the cost of utilities, like heating and electric bills; property taxes; and potential maintenance and upkeep. In some cases, the proceeds from the sale of a larger home can be used to pay off outstanding mortgage debt and cover the purchase of a smaller property.

But when it comes to going small, it's important to remember that size isn't everything—location is just as important a factor in reducing expenses through a move. Housing costs vary considerably from one neighborhood, state and region of the country to the next. For example, a one-bedroom condo located in a city could have higher property taxes, homeowners insurance and utilities than a three-bedroom house in the suburbs. Combine those expenses with potential increases to your cost of living, and scaling down could end up raising your housing costs.

If you're thinking about downsizing your living expenses, make sure to weigh all of these factors and consider how location will affect

USING A REVERSE MORTGAGE

There is one other way to control housing costs: by tapping the equity in your home through a reverse mortgage.

With a reverse mortgage, you're still responsible for paying property taxes, maintenance and insurance on the home, but the loan eliminates your monthly mortgage payments, freeing up even more cash to save or apply toward other living expenses.

Reverse mortgages come with some considerable drawbacks, though. If you want to sell the home, you'll need to pay back the loan immediately. Reverse mortgages also tend to include higher-than-average closing costs and origination fees. The maximum home equity that you can tap is capped by the U.S. Department of Housing and Urban Development (find current rates at hud.gov). By spending down that equity, you also reduce the size of your estate, leaving fewer assets for your heirs. For instance, if your children want to keep the house after your death, they must pay back the balance of the loan.

Depending upon how early you're planning to retire, a reverse mortgage might not even be an option. To qualify, you must be at least 62 years old and either own your home or be carrying a balance on your mortgage that's low enough to be paid down at closing with proceeds from the loan. For those reasons, you may want to explore a number of other options before you consider a reverse mortgage.

You may find considerable savings in moving to a smaller space.

your move. That way you can ensure that going small will actually mean big savings.

Become a Landlord (or a Roommate)

To pare down your housing costs, you might consider turning your home into a source of income by renting out a room or section of your living space. Leasing space in your house can help defray your monthly mortgage payment—or even cover it completely.

If you have a spare bedroom, you could offer short-term rentals through a platform like Airbnb. That can be a particularly lucrative option if you live in a high-tourism area. But before you post a listing, do your due diligence: Check with your city to confirm that your rental complies with local regulations and be sure you're clear on the fees—and the work—involved in sharing your home.

Homeowners with a separate living space within their house might consider renting to longer-term tenants. While becoming a landlord requires more legal and logistical oversight than home sharing, it also provides you with a more stable income.

Looking to downsize? Consider buying a property with multiple units, where you can live in one and rent out the others. If you plan on staying in your home, adding another bedroom or an apartment could be an investment that pays big dividends going forward. Remember, you'll also need to pay taxes on the money you make renting space.

A thoughtful approach to managing housing costs can be the foundation for an effective retirement plan. With a variety of solutions available, you can design a strategy that fits your family's needs and gives you the financial flexibility and the confidence to pursue your goals. ■

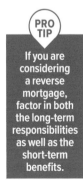

PRO TIP

If you are considering a reverse mortgage, factor in both the long-term responsibilities as well as the short-term benefits.

57

Owning vs. Renting in Retirement
Does Home Ownership Make Sense for Your Retirement?

To rent or to own? It's an eternal question in real estate. And it's one that becomes all the more important when your ability to retire early hangs in the balance. Since you may be living on a fixed income when you retire—and housing will likely be your biggest expense—it's worth spending some time considering the pros and cons of each option. Ask yourself these four questions as you weigh your options.

How Long Do I Plan to Live There

Some people wish to own their own property, create space for their personal projects and live out their days near their families. Others would prefer more flexibility with their newfound freedom. Be honest with yourself about your plans, taking into account current health care needs and future assisted-living accommodations. If you plan to move around frequently when it is considered safe to do so, it's best to rent; you're not locked into a mortgage and homeowner responsibilities while you travel. If you're looking for a place where you can settle for the next 15 to 20 years, it may be beneficial to purchase a home, since you'll have time to build additional equity.

What's the Real Estate Market Like in My Preferred Area?

You most likely have a region in mind, a desired way of life or even a specific city in which you want to live. Research the local real estate market, analyzing historic and current rental prices. Ask an expert about the economic growth of the area to gauge where prices are going. Compare this information to the cost of buying a house, taking into account home maintenance, property taxes and home insurance. For example, Florida has some of the most affordable housing when it comes to

PRO TIP

If you're buying a home for early retirement, consider future factors like accessibility and proximity to health care and family.

if you've been a two-car family but neither you nor your spouse will be commuting to work in retirement, it might be feasible to become a one-car household. Besides cashing in on the value of one of your existing cars, you'd eliminate insurance costs, vehicle registration expenses and trips to the gas station.

Saving on Insurance

Have you been using the same insurance company for years? If so, it's worth taking the time to investigate your options. When shopping around for auto insurance, ask about discounts—many companies offer discounts for having a good driving record, bundling your home and auto insurance, driving less than

Public transportation has its own rewards.

PUBLIC TRANSPORTATION: YOUR RIDE TO EARLY RETIREMENT?

The financial savings are huge, but they're not the only benefits.

By reducing the number of cars you own—or going car-free—and instead relying on public transportation, you can save plenty of money. According to the American Public Transportation Association (APTA), the savings incurred by using public transport instead of a car or truck can add up to more than $9,000 per year. By using public transport, you'll be ditching your auto insurance, vehicle maintenance costs, registration, fuel expenses, parking costs and tickets, as well as any monthly car payments you might have had.

Beyond the financial benefits, there are several other reasons to frequent public transport. Research by the APTA indicates that taking the bus, train or subway is safer than driving. It's also better for the environment and tends to improve fitness, since you'll likely be walking more to get to your stops. Plus, taking public transportation could free you up to read or catch up on emails instead of watching the road.

When you're daydreaming about places to live in retirement, don't forget to assess the public transportation in the areas you're considering. You'll want to find out how accessible an area is by public transportation—for instance, if you're moving to a suburban area, you'll need to know whether taking a bus will even be possible. Also consider how much different modes of transport cost in various locations.

You might find out that ditching your wheels improves your quality of life and lowers your expenses, to boot.

Bike-share programs are becoming more widespread.

credits for plug-in electric vehicles might help soothe the initial financial sting. Visit the energy.gov website for more information about tax incentives for electric vehicles.

average or having a car with safety features such as anti-lock brakes or anti-theft devices.

If you're already driving an older car and have a hearty emergency fund, consider minimizing your insurance. You might choose to ditch your collision coverage, which pays for repairs on an automobile in the event of a car accident, or your comprehensive coverage, which insures your vehicle against theft, natural disasters and other noncollision damage.

If the thought of being less insured makes you feel queasy but you know your car is on its last legs, another option is to raise your deductible.

Go Green

Besides being environmentally friendly, electric cars tend to incur lower expenses than nonelectric vehicles. They generally have lower maintenance and repair costs, and you'll save money by not paying for gas. Electric vehicles can be more expensive up front; however, tax

Refinance Your Car Loan

If you have a loan on your vehicle, you may be able to lower your costs by refinancing your existing loan. If interest rates have dipped or your credit score has risen since you originated your loan, refinancing could help save you money. Refinancing an auto doesn't bring the big closing costs of refinancing a mortgage; typically, the only fees involved are for transferring your title and a small lender fee. Of course, this equation assumes the balance on your loan is less than the value of your car. Alternately, if you have the room in your budget to bulk up your payments on your existing agreement, you'll save on interest over the life of your loan without being locked into a different monthly payment.

Alternatives to Car Ownership

Depending on where you live in retirement, biking, walking or using public transport or ride-sharing services, like Uber, could help you eliminate the need to own your own vehicle or even go car-free.

If it's feasible to reduce the number of cars you own, you could even use the savings to contribute to your early retirement fund while knowing your costs will be also more manageable in the future.

Cutting your auto costs now can help you coast into early retirement sooner. ∎

PRO TIP

Buying an electric car can save you money on gas and repairs. Tax incentives for electric cars can help lower the higher up-front costs.

When it comes
to controlling
your auto
costs, there
are a variety
of options.

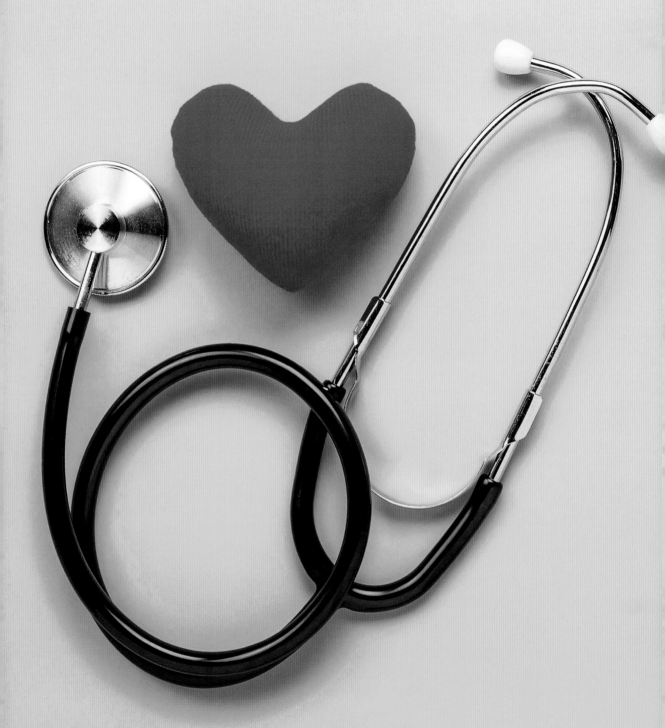

Health Care

Navigating your options
for early retirement and beyond

04 | **MEDICAL MANAGEMENT** 01 | 02 | 03 | 04 | 05 | 06

Understanding the Long-Term Costs of Your Medical Expenses
Calculating the Price of Longevity

People today are living longer than ever before. According to the Social Security Administration, the average life expectancy in the U.S. for a 65-year-old today is 87 years for women and 84 years for men. And the younger you are now, the more likely it is that you could live well beyond that. However, longer life spans means planning for more years of health care in retirement. In 2020, a healthy couple would need to have $295,000 set aside just for health care if they were to retire that year at age 65, according to Fidelity Benefits Consulting. If you plan to retire early, you'll also need to factor in the cost of that extra time. Consider these health care options to help you get through the different stages of retirement.

Early Retirement

If you retire early and no longer have employer health care coverage, you'll have to find a way to acquire coverage yourself until you qualify for Medicare at age 65. You may need to purchase private insurance through an exchange, use COBRA to extend your current plan or use a working spouse's plan. Some retirees even move to countries with low-cost health care or take up part-time jobs to stay covered before becoming eligible for Medicare.

Retirement Age

Once you're 65, you'll be eligible for Medicare. But you'll still have a number of health care costs you'll need to cover out of pocket. Medicare still comes with monthly premiums, deductibles and copays. People are often surprised to find that Medicare might not cover common needs that seniors have, like eye exams, glasses, dental work (including dentures), hearing aids and custodial care. These expenses, over the course of decades, add up quickly.

PRO TIP

Purchasing long-term-care insurance when you're relatively young can be more affordable than waiting until later in your life.

Medicare provides health care coverage to 67 million Americans.

Late Retirement

The biggest health care cost you need to plan for is likely to be long-term care. In 2013, Americans paid a total of $57.2 billion out of pocket for long-term-care services, according to the Congressional Research Service. About half of all seniors will end up paying for long-term care out of pocket. One way to avoid the high cost of long-term care is by purchasing long-term-care (LTC) insurance. LTC policies cover custodial care like long-term nursing home stays, in-home care and other services. LTC insurance plans are less expensive when you purchase them at a younger age. Purchasing a plan before you retire or early in retirement can help keep your health care costs down in the future.

Even the healthiest person today will face health issues somewhere down the line. To ensure the happy, healthy retirement you've been looking forward to, it's important to understand and plan for these costs. ■

Your insurance needs
will depend on the age at
which you plan to retire.

Health Insurance for Early Retirees
A Look at the Options for Coverage

The type of health insurance you'll have when you retire will largely depend on how old you are at the time. While some companies continue to offer employer-based health insurance to early retirees as part of their benefits package, it's not a universal practice. If your spouse is still working and has insurance through his or her employer, joining that plan may be the simplest, least expensive option for now. Barring either of these situations, finding health insurance before Medicare kicks in can be complicated.

The best course of action will depend on your age, your income and where you live. If you retire just before you turn 65, you'll only need insurance for a short time before you become eligible for Medicare. If you're retiring closer to 50, you'll need a more long-term strategy. Luckily, there are plenty of ways to make sure you stay covered, and coverage doesn't necessarily need to break the bank. Here's a look at some of your options.

COBRA

If you've been insured through an employer-based plan up to retirement, you may be eligible for COBRA, which lets you extend that plan even though you're no longer employed by the company. This should be considered a short-term fix, since generally, you can only use COBRA for 18 months. Also, be prepared for your premiums to rise sharply. When you use COBRA, you pay the full cost of the insurance, with no employer subsidy. Many retirees find that the full cost of the premium is more than they would pay if they were to seek private insurance on their own.

Health Care Exchanges

If COBRA is not an option—or is simply too costly—you can likely find insurance on either a state or federal exchange. Insurance exchanges were created under the Affordable Care Act, also known as Obamacare; visit your state's exchange website to see the plans offered through different insurance companies.

Buying insurance through the exchange means you may have access to health insurance that's subsidized based on your income. You pick your plan (though some states' options are more limited than others), but you'll benefit from seeing the most affordable plans for your income level. According to eHealth's Health Insurance Price Index, in 2020, the average unsubsidized premium for an individual between ages 55 and 64 was $784 per month.

Alternative Strategies

Many people retire early in order to spend more time doing what they love—traveling, volunteering or pursuing other passions. It's worth considering whether any of these pursuits could provide you with the health coverage you need. For example, many volunteer programs, such as the Peace Corps, provide health insurance for as long as you're working with them.

If you're not looking to volunteer but you love to travel, you may be interested in retiring or spending time in a country with significantly lower medical costs (after checking to make sure the public health situation is stable). Depending on how long you are planning to live abroad, you can purchase travel insurance that covers health care, or even potentially enroll in a local plan if you're eligible. Countries such as Mexico and Thailand provide high-quality, low-cost medical care that attracts patients from a number of other countries where care is more expensive. You can even purchase medical tourism insurance that covers unexpected complications that could arise from any medical procedures you may have while abroad. ■

PRO TIP

When purchasing from a health care exchange, you can compare premiums, deductibles and other out-of-pocket costs.

Finding affordable health insurance can be a tricky proposition for early retirees.

73

Understanding Medicare
What You Need to Know Now

The government-sponsored Medicare insurance program has helped cover health care costs for millions of Americans since President Harry Truman received the first Medicare card in 1965. Today, Medicare provides coverage to 67 million Americans, the majority of whom are over age 65. But while approximately 20 percent of the U.S. population receives Medicare benefits, many people still don't feel as though they have a strong grasp on exactly what the program is, what it provides and who is eligible to receive it under today's rules and guidelines.

People under age 65 may think they don't need to fully understand Medicare's many complexities, but even if you're not yet of the age where you are able to qualify for the program's benefits, you can still do yourself a favor by learning more about it now. That way, when the time comes to enroll, you'll have a strong grasp of the program's deadlines and the choices you have to make.

Medicare Enrollment

You'll become automatically eligible for Medicare the day you turn 65—but most people will still have to apply to make sure they get coverage. People who are already receiving Social Security benefits before they turn 65 will be automatically enrolled in Medicare Part A and B; everyone else has to enroll online. It's important to plan ahead, because there are limited windows in which you can apply for Medicare. Most people take advantage of the program's Initial Enrollment Period (IEP). That period spans seven months, beginning three months before the month in which you turn 65 and ending three months after the month you turn 65. (For example, if you were born on August 8, your initial enrollment period would begin May 1 and end November 30.) It's smart to apply for Medicare before you turn 65, as the enrollment process can take a few months to complete.

If you don't sign up during the initial enrollment period, you may face late-enrollment penalties, higher premiums and gaps in your coverage.

Even if you're not yet 65, it's a good idea to familiarize yourself with Medicare.

75

Pay attention to the filing deadlines.

However, some people—for example, those still covered by their employer's health plans or their spouse's employer's plans—choose to delay their Medicare enrollment. You can do so without facing a penalty under certain circumstances, as long as you enroll in Medicare within eight months of losing your employer health insurance; consult medicare.gov for more detailed information.

Medicare Premiums

Contrary to what some people expect, Medicare won't cover all your health care costs. You'll still have premiums and copays, just as you do for private health care coverage. There are exceptions: Medicare's low-income program, Extra Help,

covers a significant portion of prescription-drug costs for people who qualify, while some states offer Medicare Savings Programs to help low-income people cover deductibles, premiums and copays. However, if your income is above a certain threshold ($87,000 for an individual or $174,000 for a couple in 2020), you'll have to pay higher premiums for Medicare Part B and D coverage). For up-to-date information, visit medicare.gov.

Medicare Parts A–D

The Medicare program is divided into several parts that provide different kinds of coverage for different costs (or, in some cases, for no cost at all). Plans can differ in terms of cost, quality and coverage. To get full coverage, most people either opt to enroll in traditional Medicare—Medicare Parts A, B, D and Medigap coverage—or sign up for Medicare Part C, also known as Medicare Advantage, which is administered by private insurance companies that contract with the Medicare program. Before you make a choice, consider your current health care situation, your reasonable expectation of future needs, your financial situation and any other relevant information.

PART A

Medicare Part A covers hospital services, such as in-patient stays, care in a skilled-nursing facility, hospice care and, in some cases, home health care. You can enroll in Part A coverage at no cost, as long as you (or your spouse) have paid Medicare payroll taxes for at least 10 years. If you don't qualify for free Part A coverage, you'll have to pay a premium of several hundred dollars a month

PRO TIP

As you approach age 65, start familiarizing yourself with the Medicare enrollment process, including the enrollment windows.

in order to enroll. Once you meet the annual deductible, Part A will typically cover 100 percent of the costs of hospitalization up to 60 days.

PART B

Medicare Part B covers the cost of doctor's office visits and other outpatient services. Most Medicare recipients paid $144.60 a month in 2020 for their Part B premiums, according to AARP, though some Social Security recipients paid a little less, and people with high incomes paid substantially more. Once you've met the annual deductible, which increased to $198 in 2020 (check medicare.gov for the most recent figure), Part B will cover 80 percent of approved costs.

PART C

Medicare Part C is also called Medicare Advantage, and it provides health care coverage through private insurance companies. Part C plans include the same coverage as traditional Medicare Parts A and B; it may also include additional vision, hearing and dental benefits and/or prescription-drug coverage. As with traditional Medicare, enrolling in Part C coverage will mean you'll have to pay monthly premiums, and you'll be subject to deductible payments, copays and other out-of-pocket costs when you receive care. Medicare Part C plans vary widely; in general, they offer lower premiums but higher cost-sharing and a more limited choice of providers.

PART D

Medicare Part D pays for the costs of prescription drugs. The monthly premium for Part D coverage varies, depending on where you live and which plan you choose to enroll in; the average monthly premium for Part D coverage in 2020 was just over $42. Part D plans can vary quite a bit in terms of which drugs they cover and at

> # For most people, Medicare alone won't cover all of your health care costs.

what cost. Before picking a Part D plan, make sure to calculate how much you'll be paying to get your current medications through the plans you're considering.

Medigap Insurance

Medigap insurance, which is also known as Medicare supplemental insurance, exists to help fill some of the gaps in the Medicare program. Medigap insurance is purchased separately from Medicare, and it's offered by private insurance companies. Medigap insurance policies are also identified by letters—in this case, A through N. Although there may be some differences between the Medigap plans that are offered by different companies, policies with the same letter will all offer the same basic benefits. Their costs, however, will vary, depending on the company that offers them and the state in which you live. Some Medigap insurance policies include out-of-pocket maximums, while others do not.

A Complex Topic

The array of details and options involved in Medicare can make it feel daunting and overwhelming. However, help is available. Consult your local State Health Insurance Assistance Programs for unbiased one-on-one counseling and assistance. You can find your state's program at shiptacenter.org, or look for information at medicare.gov and the AARP website, aarp.org/health/medicare-insurance. ∎

Paying for Prescription Drugs
Dealing With the High Costs

The cost of prescription drugs is one of the biggest expenses you may face in retirement. You have a number of options—including Medicare—that can help you cover the cost of the medicines you need. But not every medication is covered by every plan—and retirees who aren't old enough for Medicare must find other ways to pay for medication.

Medicare: What It Covers, What It Doesn't

Medicare has multiple parts, each with different costs and areas of coverage. Medicare Part D covers medications. Those enrolled in Part D pay a monthly premium and a copay or a cost-sharing portion for medications. There are a number of Part D options, each with a different price and covered drugs. The average monthly premium for a Part D plan was just over $42 in 2020.

The Medicare website helps you see the options available in your area, at medicare.gov/find-a-plan. Before you enroll in a plan, consult its formulary to see if the drugs you need will be covered and how much they'll cost.

Make sure to include both the cost of medication and the monthly premium when you're calculating which plan will work best for you. Low-income people who qualify for Medicare should investigate Medicare's Extra Help program, which assists eligible participants with the cost of prescription-drug plans.

Retirees can also enroll in a Medicare Advantage plan, also known as Medicare Part C. These comprehensive plans are comparable to Medicare options, but they're offered by private insurers. Many Medicare Advantage plans offer prescription-drug coverage, but again the plans vary in terms of coverage and costs.

Beware the Donut Hole

People with prescription coverage through Medicare Part D should be aware of the coverage

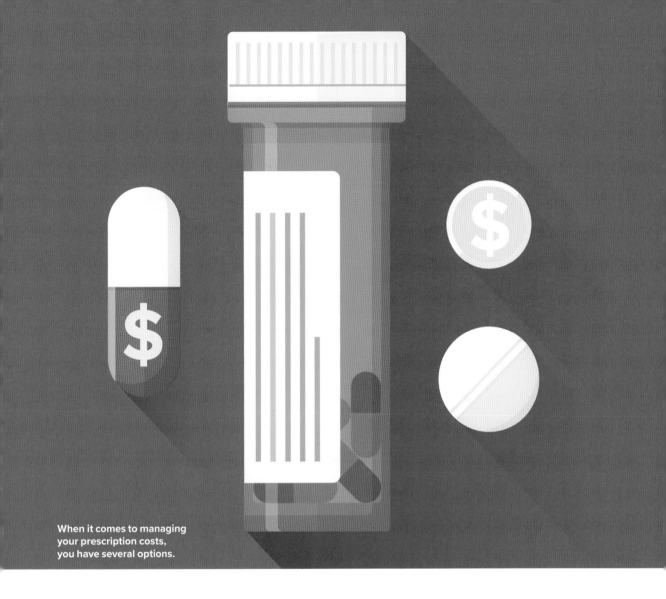

When it comes to managing your prescription costs, you have several options.

gap, also called the donut hole. If your prescription costs are below a certain threshold ($4,020 in 2020), some of your drug costs will be covered. Drug costs above that amount will be your responsibility. However, you'll receive a 75 percent "donut hole discount" on brand-name drugs until your out-of-pocket costs reach the annual limit ($6,350 in 2020; check medicare.gov for up-to-date information). At that point, the Part D drug plan will kick in to cover your prescriptions. This new process reflects the accelerated closing of the donut hole, enacted as part of a budget deal signed in early 2018.

Other Ways to Cover Medication Costs

Early retirees are likely not yet eligible for Medicare and will therefore have to find another strategy for paying for their medication expenses. Some organizations will continue to extend health benefits to early retirees until they reach the age when they're eligible for Medicare. Other early retirees may have to rely upon a spouse's health benefits. If those aren't options for you, you can also explore the plans that are offered to individuals in each state on the health care exchange. (For information, visit healthcare.gov.) ■

Planning for the future now can save you money and ease your mind.

The Role of Long-Term-Care Insurance
Preparing Now to Cover Future Health Care Costs

Health insurance—whether it's Medicare or a plan you purchased on your own through the health insurance marketplace—will cover many, but not all your retirement medical costs. Critically, Medicare and other health care insurance policies do not cover long-term care, including assistance with day-to-day tasks. Whether due to chronic illness, disability or old age, many people late in their lives need help with basic tasks like bathing, dressing and eating. Long-term-care insurance helps you shoulder the costs of help from nurses, therapists and other medical professionals. It can help with in-home care, as well as with services provided at assisted living facilities and nursing homes.

If you're planning to retire early, the time when you might need long-term care may seem too far away to think about now. But 70 percent of people need long-term care at some point in their lives, a figure that may grow as average life spans continue to increase. And long-term care can be very expensive. Consider that the average cost of a semiprivate room in a nursing home is $6,844 per month, according to the U.S. Department of Health and Human Services. If you fail to plan for the possibility now, you risk struggling to afford the care you might need when you're older.

What Long-Term-Care Insurance Covers

Different long-term-care insurance policies cover different costs. If you have an idea of the kind of care you'll need—if you have a chronic illness, for example—be sure to choose a policy that will provide for that care. If, like many people, you don't know what services you might need, try to choose a policy with some built-in flexibility.

Long-term care typically provides access to nursing homes, which provide

PRO TIP

Long-term-care insurance benefits may include adult day care, home modifications, and assisted living and nursing home stays.

around-the-clock care along with room and board. They also cover assisted-living facilities, which provide an apartment and access to care as needed. Medicare covers short stays in nursing homes or assisted-living facilities or a limited amount of at-home care. Most long-term-care insurance policies pay for more extended care.

Some policies also pay for adult day care, which helps relieve the daily burden on caregivers by providing medical care and social opportunities during the day. Many insurance companies require plan participants to use services from a certified home-care agency or licensed professional. Others give you the option of hiring independent care providers or even family members.

Some policies will also cover home modifications such as ramps, remodeled bathrooms and enlarged doorways. If you want a plan that covers you and your partner or another family member, you might consider buying a joint policy. Joint policies typically cap their benefits at a predetermined amount that is available to both of the insured parties.

When to Buy Long-Term-Care Insurance

The right time to buy long-term-care insurance depends on your current health and financial situation as well as your financial outlook. Generally speaking, it's better to buy earlier rather than later, since policies cost less when you're younger and in good health.

If you wait until your health is showing signs of decline, long-term-care insurance will almost certainly cost more—if you can find coverage at all. If you have a preexisting condition, some insurers may turn you down, while others will withhold payment for care related to that condition for a certain amount of time after you buy the policy. Don't fail to mention a preexisting

condition, though. If your insurer finds out about it after the fact, the company may revoke your coverage.

If you're not sure you can afford long-term-care insurance, ask your financial adviser to help you make a plan. Keep in mind that any benefits you receive from your policy aren't taxed as income. Also be aware that your insurer may raise your plan's premium—so be sure you understand the terms before you sign a policy. Adding inflation protection can help you keep up with the costs of health care as your retirement progresses.

How to Buy Long-Term-Care Insurance

If your current employer offers long-term-care plans, consider buying one before you retire. Many such plans are available at a discount. If you leave your job or your employer decides to stop providing the benefit, you can usually still hold on to the policy as long as you continue to pay the premiums.

If an employer-sponsored plan is not available to you, see if you have access to a group-rate plan from a professional or service organization you belong to. If not, you can buy a policy through an insurance agent or broker. Make sure the person you buy from has had training in long-term-care insurance and is licensed to sell insurance in your state.

Long-term-care insurance may not seem like a priority when you're considering early retirement and are in relatively good health. But preparing for it now can help you to avoid difficult financial realities later— plus you'll rest easier knowing your care will be provided for, well into the future. ∎

PRO TIP

Long-term-care insurance can be purchased through employers, professional organizations or an insurance professional.

Consider purchasing long-term-care insurance early, while you're in good health.

When considering medical tourism, learn your options for follow-up care.

Medical Tourism
Taking Your Health Care on the Road

Managing health care costs can be a challenge for early retirees. Without coverage through an employer and with years to go before becoming eligible for Medicare, early retirees are responsible for finding and paying for their own health insurance.

Potentially expensive premiums aren't the only concern. If you need a major medical procedure, deductibles and out-of-pocket costs can eat up a considerable amount of your savings and derail your carefully laid plans. That's why early retirees, given safe travel conditions, might consider having medical procedures performed outside the U.S., where more affordable health care costs can mean big savings. Though still in its early stages, medical tourism has become an increasingly popular trend. In 2017, an estimated 1.4 million Americans traveled abroad for treatment, according to consumer information group Patients Beyond Borders.

Medical tourism can deliver quality care at a fraction of the cost so you can receive the treatment you need without jeopardizing your retirement timeline or long-term goals. But not all overseas medical options are created equal, and there are factors to consider when determining whether traveling for health care is the right choice.

The Benefits of Medical Tourism

Today, Americans travel around the world for medical treatments like orthopedic and cardiovascular surgery, oncology and dentistry. Medical tourism provides patients with access to attractive destinations, high-quality services and, in some cases, procedures and medications that are otherwise unavailable domestically. But maybe the most compelling benefit is the savings it can provide.

Some of the most popular destinations, including India, Brazil, Malaysia and Thailand, offer services at costs between 20 percent and

85

90 percent lower than they would be in the U.S. A CT scan that costs $800 in the U.S. could run about $300 in Costa Rica—and an office visit with a specialist could be as low as $20.

Savings on routine procedures are a welcome relief to any patient. But for those who could save up to $30,000 on a hip replacement or $50,000 on an angioplasty by having major surgery abroad, the potential value of medical tourism is far more significant. That's especially true for those who need to minimize expenses ahead of an early retirement.

Medical tourism allows patients to limit their expenses without sacrificing quality of service or their well-being. Thanks to clean, modern facilities and experienced practitioners—many of whom have trained in other countries, including the U.S.—the treatment patients can receive abroad is on par with, and in some cases may even be superior to, the medical care that they might receive at home.

Important Considerations

While there can be myriad benefits to seeking medical treatment in another country, not all medical-tourism experiences are created equal, so there are important considerations for patients to think about before they undergo treatment.

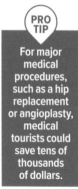

PRO TIP

For major medical procedures, such as a hip replacement or angioplasty, medical tourists could save tens of thousands of dollars.

While many popular medical-tourism countries have highly rated health systems, it's important to look beyond those rankings into the specific hospitals and clinics where procedures will actually be performed. This is where things can get tricky: Standards for foreign

About 1.4 million Americans traveled abroad for health treatments in 2017.

practitioners and medical facilities are often different from those in the U.S., which can make evaluating them a bit of a challenge. However, a number of organizations, including the Joint Commission International, The International Society for Quality in Health Care and DNV International Healthcare Accreditation, provide vetting and accreditation of facilities.

Language can also be a challenge. Most hospitals participating in medical tourism have English-speaking staff, or at the very least offer translators. Still, language barriers make careful communication between patients and caregivers extremely important.

Another issue is follow-up care—or the lack thereof. Should a complication occur once a patient has returned home from a procedure performed abroad, they no longer have direct access to the practitioner who performed it. The American College of Surgeons recommends that medical-tourism participants obtain a complete set of medical records before returning home in order to facilitate effective continuity of care once they're back stateside.

Given the potential advantages and risks, medical tourism is an option early retirees in need of expensive medical services should consider carefully as travel restrictions ease. A trip abroad just might help cut expenses so that you and your retirement plan stay in tip-top shape. ∎

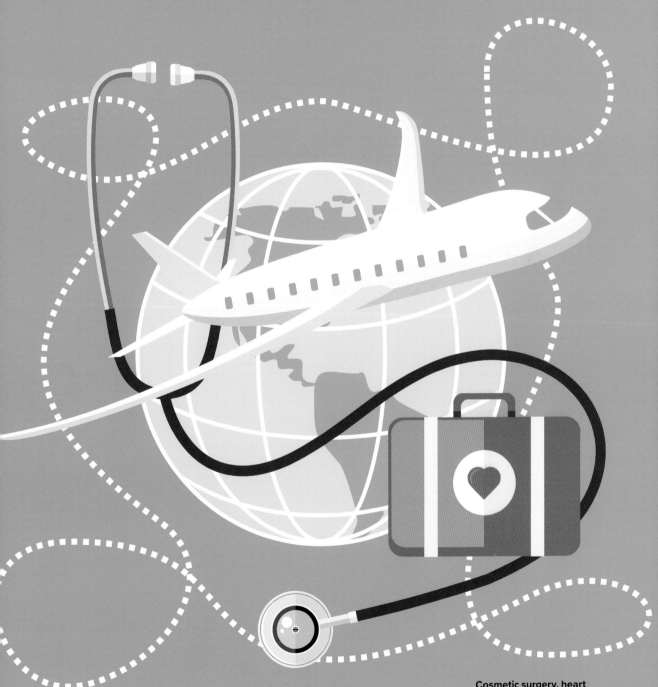

Cosmetic surgery, heart surgery and dentistry are the most common medical tourism procedures.

Building Your Savings

Laying the groundwork for early retirement

05 COMPOUNDING   01 | 02 | 03 | 04 | 05 | 06 | 07 | 08

The Power of Compounding
Harness Time to Grow Your Savings

Think of compound interest as a way to supercharge your savings. The earlier you start saving, the more time you have to take advantage of its magical power—and the better positioned you'll be to retire on your own terms.

Of course, there isn't anything actually magical about the concept of compounding. The fundamental principle underlying compound interest is simple: When your investments earn money and you reinvest those earnings, your savings then have the potential to grow exponentially over time.

Over years, even a small savings account has the power to grow into a serious nest egg, thanks to compounding. If your savings are invested inside a tax-free vehicle, such as a Roth IRA, the effects of compounding will be even more powerful, because you won't be taxed on the growth of your investments. Tax-deferred vehicles, such as traditional IRAs and 401(k)s, allow your investments to grow tax-free, although you will have to pay income tax on withdrawals.

To see how powerful compounding can be, imagine that you took $50 from your biweekly paycheck at age 30 and invested it in an account with a 6 percent annual rate of return. By the time you turned 65, you would have amassed nearly $150,000. If you'd waited 15 years and started saving at age 45, your savings would be significantly lower—just under $100,000—even if you doubled your biweekly contribution to $100.

It bears repeating: Saving early and often are the two best ways to benefit from compounding. The earlier you start—and the earlier you take advantage of compounding's supercharge effect—the faster you'll reach your early-retirement goals. ∎

PRO TIP

Consider investing in a tax-free savings vehicle, such as a Roth IRA, to stretch the power of compound interest even further.

Time plus reinvested
interest can create
exponential returns.

Get the Most Out of Your Retirement Savings Accounts
Maximize Tax-Deferred Funds and Employer Contributions

No matter when you plan to retire, tax-advantaged retirement plans can be a huge boost to your savings. The most common plans, 401(k)s and IRAs, offer similar benefits—but there are important differences. And when you factor in the Roth versions of 401(k)s and IRAs, your savings options multiply.

Maximizing your tax-advantaged savings won't get you all the way to your early retirement goals—but you should still make the most of them, as they offer tax breaks that your other savings options may not provide. Start by familiarizing yourself with the ins and outs of each type of plan. Then, using your overall retirement strategy as a guide, consider switching plans, adding a new one or making adjustments to your current plan.

> **PRO TIP**
>
> If you're over 50, you can use catch-up contributions to stash as much as an extra $6,500 in your 401(k) or 403(b) and $7,000 in your IRA.

Employer-Sponsored Plans

If your employer offers a 401(k) (or a 403(b) or 457, which are similar), aim to max out your retirement savings. For anyone under 50, the 2020 annual contribution limit is $19,500. Those 50 and older can contribute an extra $6,500 per year, for a total of $26,000. For up-to-date figures, visit irs.gov. All the income you contribute to a 401(k) is tax-deferred, and funds in the 401(k) compound tax-free. You will have to pay income tax on the withdrawals you take from the plan in retirement. You can start withdrawing from 401(k)s at age 59½, and you are required to take minimum distributions starting at age 70½. If you withdraw from your 401(k) before age 59½, you'll be subject to a 10 percent penalty in addition to income tax on the withdrawal.

Many employers offer matching contributions to a 401(k), up to a certain percentage of your salary. If your employer offers matching contributions, take advantage of them. If you don't, you're essentially passing up free money. Be

Matching contributions are essentially free money; take advantage of them.

sure you're clear on your employer's vesting schedule, which typically dictates when you take ownership of employer-matching contributions. Depending on when you plan to leave your job, this schedule can have a major impact on how much of those contributions you can actually keep.

Traditional IRAs

Anyone under the age of 70½ is allowed to contribute to a traditional individual retirement account, or IRA. Contributions to traditional IRAs are generally tax-deductible, although the deduction may be limited if you (or your spouse) are covered by a workplace retirement plan and your modified adjusted gross income (MAGI) exceeds certain levels. For example, in 2020, deductions phased out for single filers with MAGI between $65,000 and $75,000 and for joint filers with MAGI between $104,000 and $124,000.

As with 401(k)s, your investments grow tax-free, you cannot start withdrawing before age 59½

without a 10 percent penalty and you must take required minimum distributions at age 70½. The contribution limits are significantly lower for traditional IRAs, however: $6,000, for people under 50; and $7,000, for people 50 and older.

The Roth Options

Roth IRAs and Roth 401(k)s offer different tax advantages from their traditional counterparts. Contributions to Roth retirement accounts are made with after-tax dollars, meaning you can't deduct them. However, withdrawals are penalty- and tax-free, so long as you've held the account at least five years and are 59½ or older. Early withdrawals are subject to a 10 percent penalty, with some exceptions. Contribution limits to Roth plans are the same as traditional plans (including catch-up options). Not all employers that offer 401(k)s provide Roth options. When choosing between a traditional and a Roth plan, a Roth might be a better choice if you're in a lower tax bracket now than you expect to be in when you retire.

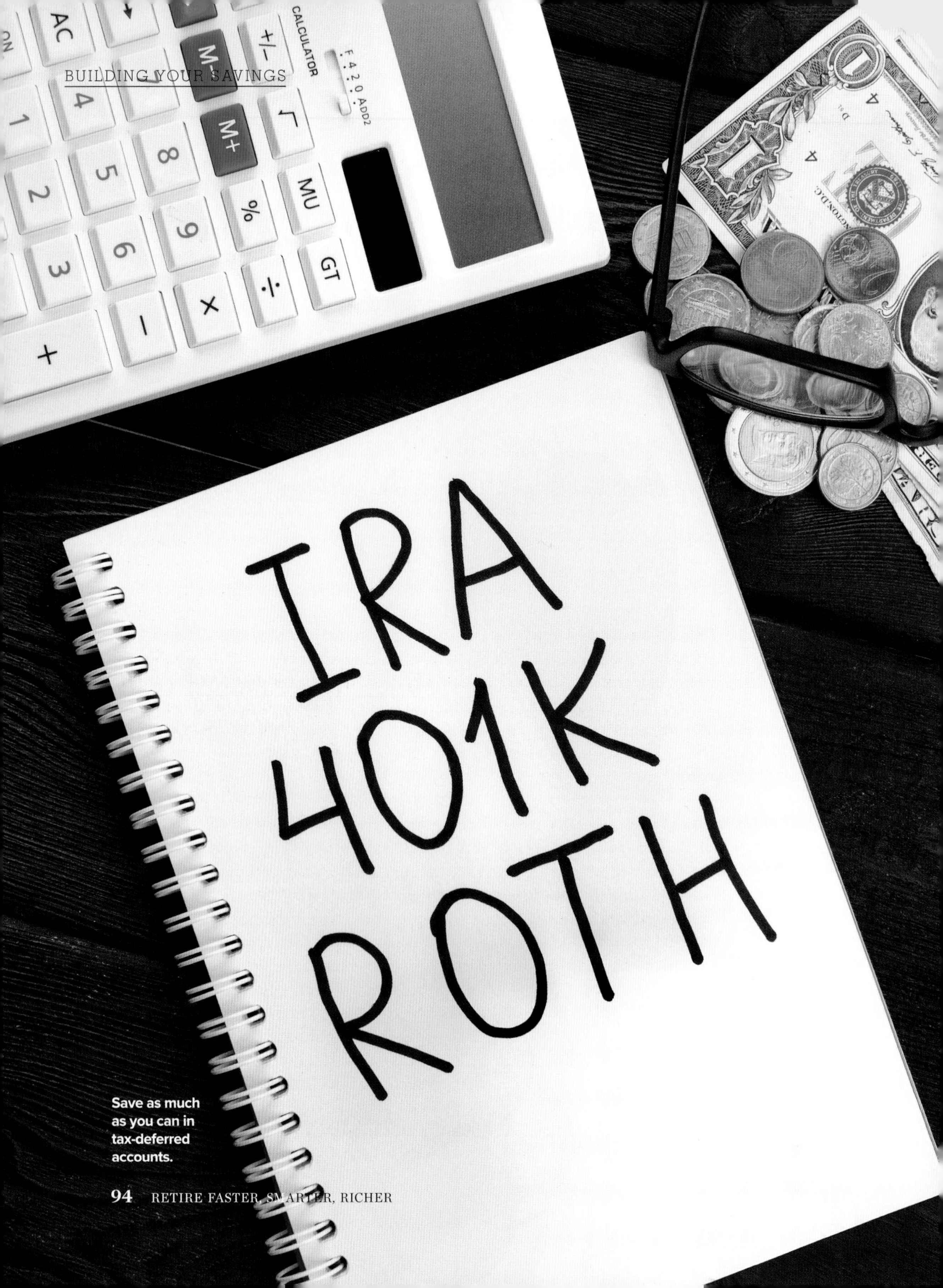

IRA
401K
ROTH

Save as much
as you can in
tax-deferred
accounts.

There are no required minimum distributions with Roth plans, and you can continue contributing to a Roth account in your 70s and beyond—providing you have earned income and meet eligibility requirements. Note that high-income earners are limited in their ability to fund Roth accounts. The ability to make Roth contributions phases out for couples with a 2020 MAGI of $196,000 to $206,000 and for single filers with a MAGI of $124,000 to $139,000. Again, visit irs.gov for the latest figures.

Options for Self-Employed Workers and Small Business Owners

Self-employed workers and small business owners can invest in traditional or Roth IRAs, but there are other options that may serve them better, depending on their situation. Those with no employees might consider a solo 401(k), which—like other 401(k)s—offers a higher contribution limit than IRAs: $57,000 for 2020. That figure includes the amount you can contribute in your capacity as both employee and employer (of yourself). As with standard 401(k)s, your contributions are tax-deductible and withdrawals after age 59½ are taxed.

SEP IRAs offer the same tax advantages and high contribution limits as solo 401(k)s, and they come with fewer administrative responsibilities. However, SEP IRAs may allow smaller annual contributions at identical income levels, due to the way the annual contribution is calculated. Also consider that, unlike solo 401(k)s, SEP IRAs do not offer catch-up contributions.

Another option for the self-employed and for business owners with as many as 100 employees is a SIMPLE IRA. You can contribute up to 100 percent of your net self-employment earnings to a SIMPLE IRA, up to $13,500 (plus a catch-up contribution of $3,000, if you're 50 or older), in 2020. Employers are required to contribute an additional 2 percent or 3 percent of employee compensation. Contributions are tax-free; withdrawals after age 59½ are taxed.

Mixing-and-Matching Plans

There are no rules that limit you to a single retirement plan. In fact, contributing to two accounts is great to maximize tax-advantaged savings. One option is to contribute to both a 401(k) and a Roth IRA. That way, you get tax-deferred savings on up to $25,000 per year, if you're 50 or over, plus you can count on a hefty chunk of tax-free income when you start withdrawing from your Roth account. If you don't have access to a 401(k), you can contribute to both a traditional IRA and a Roth IRA, but your combined contributions can't exceed the $6,000 annual limit ($7,000, for those 50 or older).

Strategies for Making Contributions

Your employer can help you manage workplace plan contributions—and, in fact, may have already automatically enrolled you in the plan. Your contributions will be deducted from your paycheck, meaning you won't even have a chance to spend that cash before it hits your savings.

You can also set up regular transfers to any retirement accounts you don't hold with your employer, rather than waiting until the tax-filing deadline to make a single large contribution. And remember: Maximizing tax-advantaged retirement savings means that your money is working harder for your future while you prepare to stop working and enjoy your freedom. ■

PRO TIP

Expect to be in a higher tax bracket in retirement? It may make sense to choose a Roth IRA over a traditional IRA, to lower your taxes later.

05 EMERGENCY FUND   01 | 02 | 03 | 04 | 05 | 06 | 07 | 08

Build an Emergency Fund
Create a Buffer for Unexpected Expenses

We've all been taught to save for a rainy day. Yet more than 60 percent of Americans don't have enough in savings to cover even a $1,000 emergency. So when the furnace needs replacing or you face an unexpected trip to the emergency room, how will you pay that bill?

One option is to pull out your credit card. But an emergency charged today on your credit card could take years to pay off—with interest being tacked on all the while. It also can be tempting to tap into retirement savings. But withdrawing that money prematurely can mean a big chunk of it goes toward paying taxes and penalties. What's more, drawing down these account balances could mean pushing back on your retirement dreams.

The good news: Establishing an emergency fund allows you to save for life's curveballs without creating more debt or jeopardizing your early-retirement plans.

Building an Emergency Fund

Ideally, your emergency fund should cover between three to six months' worth of living expenses. If you don't have steady employment or if a new job could be difficult get, you may want to save more than six months' worth of expenses.

Keep your emergency fund in an easily accessible place, such as a bank savings account. You also might consider stashing your savings in a money market account or a short-term bond fund, to earn additional interest. But the goal is to be able to quickly access your savings, so focus more on liquidity than the interest rate your savings will earn.

Stick to a Strategy

Building an emergency fund can take some time, so it pays to start early. Look for opportunities to add to your fund on a regular basis. For instance,

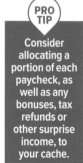

PRO TIP

Consider allocating a portion of each paycheck, as well as any bonuses, tax refunds or other surprise income, to your cache.

you might set up an automatic transfer of a portion of each paycheck into a savings account or funnel part of your income-tax refund into your emergency fund. Together, those regular and occasional contributions will add up.

Bear in mind that you don't need to set aside your other savings goals in order to get your emergency fund up and running. Instead, you can divide your cash among your savings goals—and know that you're making progress toward all of them.

And remember, you don't need to have three to six months' worth of savings before your emergency fund can come in handy. Saving just $100 per month will leave you with $1,200 at the end of the year. That may not be enough to live on for three months, but it can help cover an emergency like a sudden car repair or a leaky roof. Best of all, having money saved for life's unexpected surprises can help keep you focused on pursuing some of your long-term financial goals, such as retiring early and on your own terms. ■

Having an emergency fund protects you financially from life's curveballs.

Eliminating high-interest debt can propel you toward your savings goals.

Dealing With Debt
Crafting a Plan to Eliminate Monies Owed

To many people, debt and investments occupy different planets—and the investment planet has a stronger gravitational pull. The impulse to prioritize savings over debt payments is understandable: It can be more satisfying to grow a large sum of money than to bring a debt you owe closer to zero. But the long-term financial impact of paying down your debts—especially the high-interest ones—is probably greater than you think.

At first blush, a person's assets and debts are quite different. One represents total dollars; the other represents total negative dollars. But in virtually all cases, the two sums share an important characteristic: They're accumulating interest. That means they are both locked into a pattern of annual compounding that can strongly affect your bottom line over time. Viewed in this light (and controlling for taxes and other factors), the question of what to focus on boils down to which has a higher interest rate. Here's a look at how to deal with debt so you can build your savings faster.

Spend to Save

For an apples-to-apples comparison, say Lisa carries a credit card balance of $5,000, accruing 10 percent annual interest fees, and a Roth IRA balance of $5,000 producing about 7 percent annual returns. Lisa just got a $1,000 year-end bonus and wants to spend it as responsibly as possible, but she isn't sure whether that means lopping off $1,000 in card debt or investing $1,000 in one of her retirement accounts.

When you compare the compounding effects of both options, it's a clear answer: The card balance has a higher rate, so she should use the money to lower her debt. Consider that after one year, $1,000 off her debt would cut $100 (or 10 percent) in credit card interest. By contrast, $1,000 extra in her Roth IRA would drive about $70 (or 7 percent) in investment returns.

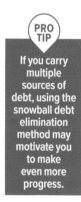

PRO TIP

If you carry multiple sources of debt, using the snowball debt elimination method may motivate you to make even more progress.

That may be only a $30 difference but as time goes by, the gap will only widen. After five years, the $1,000 would save Lisa more than $600 in card interest and gain only about $400 in Roth returns. Setting aside the emotional benefit of a lowered debt burden, Lisa's bottom line will be about $200 higher in five years, which is $200 more she could put into her Roth. In the long run, she'll come out ahead in growing her nest egg.

What's more, Lisa's return on trimming her credit card balance is guaranteed, while the return on her Roth IRA is anything but. Investment earnings can vary widely depending on the market. If Lisa puts her money in the Roth, its return could exceed that of the debt repayment—but it could also go down, since investing in the market always brings some risk.

If you want to get a leg up on retirement but you carry consumer debt, use savings to pay down your debt balances. Of course, you should do this only if you have an adequate emergency fund. Focus on building that safety net if you don't; then you can take a closer look at your options to free up cash for extra debt payments.

Note that ordinary savings and investments aren't your only resource—you might also borrow from cash-value life insurance, if you hold a policy, or take out a home-equity loan with a low interest rate. Use this strategy with extreme caution, as it essentially means trading one debt for another. Move ahead only if you can substantially reduce the interest that accumulates on your balance for the remaining duration of the loan—and if you have the discipline to avoid running up additional debt in the meantime.

PRO TIP

The avalanche method of debt repayment works well for those who want to pay their highest-interest debt off as soon as possible.

Avalanche vs. Snowball

Opinions differ on the best strategy for paying off multiple high-interest-debt balances. Two popular approaches are the "avalanche" and "snowball" methods. As the names imply, one is about making the most immediate impact, and the other is about gradually building momentum.

When a person uses the avalanche method, they list their balances, from highest rate to lowest rate, then concentrate on paying the highest-rate ones first. When a person uses the snowball method, they order the balances from smallest to largest and pay them off in that order.

From a strictly rational viewpoint, the avalanche method is better, because it wipes out the maximum amount of interest during the time it takes to pay off all debt. But our mind isn't strictly rational. That's why many people benefit more from the snowball method. Rather than putting interest above all, the snowball method prioritizes quick wins, since you'll likely get the first balance or two off your plate in a few months. The boost you'll get from reaching that goal can help motivate you to keep going until you've eliminated every balance, even if it means paying a slightly larger sum of interest when all is said and done.

The best method depends on each person, of course. You may opt for a strategy that falls somewhere in between—say, paying off the smallest two or three balances first, then leaping to the highest-rate balances from there.

Whichever approach you take, know that paying down those balances is one of the most powerful things you can do to make progress toward an early retirement. Stacking another $100 on your monthly credit card payments may not feel like a hot investment, but it's all but guaranteed to lift your bottom line and speed your progress toward the day you can finally retire. ∎

Consumer debt is a common obstacle for hopeful early retirees.

101

Start a Health Savings Account
A Tax-Advantaged Tool for Medical Expenses

Whether it's one unexpected trip to the emergency room or managing a long-term medical condition, medical expenses can wreak havoc on your financial plans, whether they happen today or in your retirement years. Even if you're in good health now, your health care costs are likely to rise a good deal over the course of your retirement. There is some good news, though: You may be able to use a health savings account to not only minimize your out-of-pocket medical costs but also continue to save toward retirement.

What Is a Health Savings Account (HSA)?

Health savings accounts, or HSAs, are specialized savings accounts designed to offer a tax-advantaged way to cover out-of-pocket medical expenses. Contributions are made pretax (or are tax-deductible, if made outside of payroll deductions), and you can make tax-free withdrawals to pay for qualified medical expenses such as doctor-visit copays, prescription costs and hospital stays. Using HSA savings to cover medical expenses can effectively discount the overall cost, since every dollar spent hasn't been reduced by taxes.

Not all withdrawals can be made tax-free, however. If HSA withdrawals are used for nonqualified expenses, you'll owe income tax on those withdrawals and may face an early-withdrawal penalty if funds are taken out before age 65. To qualify for an HSA, you must have a high-deductible health care plan with annual deductibles of at least $1,400 for individuals in 2020 ($2,800, for families). Visit irs.gov for the latest figures.

The HSA Retirement Advantage

HSAs can help make medical expenses more affordable and also play a critical role in your retirement-planning strategy. Unlike the use-it-or-lose-it provisions of flexible spending accounts (FSAs), HSAs allow your savings and

HSA contributions can be used to pay for prescriptions, copays and more.

earnings to accumulate from year to year. For early retirees, knowing you've got a pot of money that is already set aside for health-care costs may help ease any worries about leaving your current employer's health insurance plan behind you.

HSAs are very similar to traditional IRAs: Contributions are made pretax or are tax-deductible, and earnings will grow without any taxes being taken out. The added benefit of an HSA is the tax-free withdrawal for qualified medical expenses. In 2020, an individual could contribute $3,550, while the family plan contribution limit was $7,100; those older than 55 could contribute an additional $1,000 to their accounts. Again, go to irs.gov for up-to-date numbers.

How to Start and Use an HSA

Check with your health insurance provider to see if your plan qualifies for an HSA. If it doesn't, you can still open one through a bank or credit union. Once your account is set up, you'll receive a debit card or checks that are linked to your HSA balance to pay for qualified medical expenses.

HSAs are powerful tools to mitigate medical costs and save for your future. A little preplanning now can make all the difference in the long run and ensure that your retirement years are exactly what you dreamed of. ∎

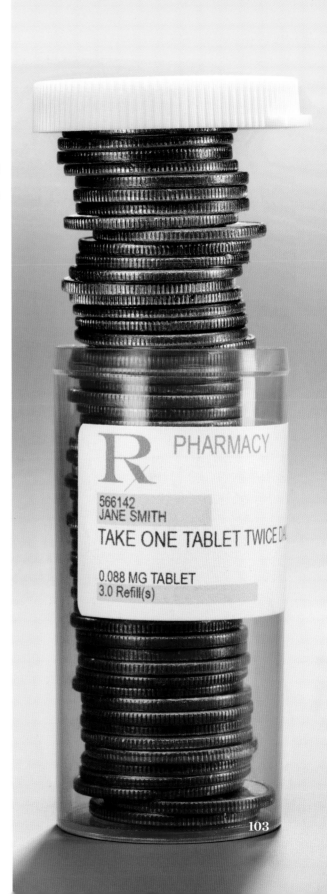

PHARMACY

566142
JANE SMITH

TAKE ONE TABLET TWICE DA

0.088 MG TABLET
3.0 Refill(s)

Turn a hobby into
a side business to
stash extra cash.

How to Start Your Side Hustle
Bulk Up Your Savings by Taking On a New Gig

Building up your savings is a lot easier when you have some extra income to work with, but your regular paycheck may be a static number that's not likely to grow.

To pad your savings more quickly, think about pursuing a side gig on top of your main source of income. This secondary job might be closely related to your current career, or it could even be a welcome change of pace from what you are now doing. A side hustle allows you to explore some different work options. If you've always worked for someone else, you can see what it's like to be your own boss. If you're tied to a desk in your 9-to-5, you can try a job that gets you on your feet.

A side hustle is good for your wallet now, but it could also provide you with some extra cash during retirement. You can start by moonlighting or working weekends while you're still at your day job. While some side gigs might be better deferred until public health challenges subside,

many can be done remotely from a home or office. Some side jobs to consider:

Join the Gig Economy

One of the perks of the gig economy, which relies on independent contractors instead of full-time employees, is that you can choose your own workload and schedule. You can even turn your car into a moneymaking machine by giving rides, making deliveries or running errands through companies such as Lyft, Uber, Instacart or Postmates. Just make sure to follow local social distancing guidelines as needed.

Teach, Consult or Coach

You've spent years collecting knowledge that has helped you in your personal and professional life. As a teacher or consultant, you can parlay that expertise into a second act. Work in the classroom or online as a substitute teacher, or one-on-one as a tutor. Develop a course on a subject you know well and offer it online

105

through Skillshare. If you'd prefer to get away from the desk, try coaching or refereeing kids' or adult rec-league sports.

Learn a New Skill

Become a florist, baker or barista. Don't be deterred by a job you've never done before. Lots of companies provide on-the-job training, and your new skills could open the door to more opportunities (and even health insurance).

Turn Your Hobby Into Cash

Knitting, ceramics or woodworking may have solely been one of your hobbies. But you might find a market for your arts and crafts when you start your own Etsy shop. Or, if you'd like to downsize your collection of vinyl records or classic books, consider becoming a seller on eBay or Amazon. And if you love to refurbish a good thrift-store find, try your hand at reselling those items online.

Get a Retail Job

Stock shelves or work as a cashier at your favorite grocery store or bookstore. If you love camping or outdoor sports, share your tips on the sales floor of a sporting-goods store. Pick a place where you shop often, so you'll get the additional perks of an employee discount.

PRO TIP
Supplement your savings by offering online classes, launching a consulting gig or selling handmade crafts on Etsy.

Be a Friendly Face

Many businesses need part-time workers in guest services, a position that's ideal if you love chatting and hospitality. Try working the front desk at a museum, health club or spa. Or share your local knowledge as a hotel concierge.

Head for the Outdoors

If mowing lawns and pruning trees is your meditation, work on the grounds crew for a golf course or your city parks. Or offer your services to neighbors and small businesses.

Become a House Sitter

Pick up the mail, water the plants and keep an eye on things when your neighbors are gone. If you live in a community where homeowners are often gone for months at a time during the summer or winter, offer your services as a caretaker who'll keep their house safe, clean and functional while owners are away. If you can build up enough regular clients, you might even be able to ditch your permanent residence (and save a bundle along the way).

Tackle Administrative Tasks

You may have already picked up key skills needed for office work, like data entry, billing and working a phone system. Check hospitals and colleges for departments that are often hiring, or browse online job postings to become a virtual assistant.

Work With Pets

If you have a way with animals, try walking dogs or pet-sitting for friends and neighbors whose pets are alone while they're at work or on vacation. Shelters, boarding kennels and groomers sometimes also have similar positions available. Added bonus: You'll get some fresh air and exercise while you work.

A side gig can take many different forms, depending on your interests and current obligations. If you earmark this extra cash for savings and watch it grow, it could be the boost you need to retire on your own schedule. ■

Dog lover?
Try pet-sitting
or dog-walking
for extra cash
(and exercise).

107

05   **PASSIVE INCOME**   01 | 02 | 03 | 04 | 05 | 06 | 07 | 08

The Benefits of Passive Income
Letting Your Money Do the Work, So You Don't Have To

As we age, we realize that time is more valuable than money. However, money is necessary to free up time—a classic chicken-and-egg scenario. Creating sources of passive income—money that you earn automatically with very little maintenance—can help you cover your financial needs in retirement, granting you time to focus on the things you love.

And while there are countless credible sources of passive income, it's important to be aware of scams in this digital age. Be wary of any sales pitches that guarantee money with no effort; most sources require significant time and energy on the front end in order to reap benefits later.

Real Estate

If you have the cash, consider buying a rental property to bring in a steady flow of income each month. Rental properties also provide an opportunity for tax deductions: interest payments on loans used to acquire or improve the rental, necessary repairs, travel resulting from rental activity, and/or depreciation. The property is essentially a business expense, so the investor can write off a portion of the cost each year for the duration of the property's recovery period, which is predetermined by the IRS.

If you have the space in your home, think about renting out a room through sites like Airbnb or Vrbo to make extra cash without the commitment of buying another house. (Just be sure that you're in compliance with local regulations about short-term rentals first.) Work with an accountant to ensure you are taking advantage of all possible deductions pertaining to your real estate assets.

Online Income

Thanks to the internet, retirees can earn money online. Blogs and websites are great ways to share specialized knowledge with the public—and make money doing it. If you've had a career

If you have the cash, buying a rental property can provide a steady flow of income.

in a niche field and you understand search engine optimization and social media marketing, you can begin generating followers for your content. If enough people regularly view your page, companies will pay to advertise on your site.

The same goes for online courses, audiobooks and e-books. Share your expertise—and earn royalties each time your book or course is downloaded. These business ventures do take time to set up, but the benefits of affiliate marketing and automatic royalties can be worth the work.

Beware of Scams

The internet provides numerous platforms to earn passive income, but it's also rife with scams. Some companies take advantage of people, leading them to believe they can make serious money in a short period of time and with little effort. Research the credibility of any business that claims to help you earn passive income—and know that all meaningful and sustainable business ventures will require some effort. For more information, contact the Federal Trade Commission at ftc.gov. ∎

05 | **GROW SAVINGS** | 01 | 02 | 03 | 04 | 05 | 06 | 07 | 08

Simple Steps to Grow Your Savings Faster
Smart Strategies for Now and Later

Big or small, the steps you take to save money are key to reaching your financial goals. The best savers employ a variety of strategies and try not to spend money needlessly. Here are some ideas to help you find places where you can increase your savings:

Bank Your Raises

It's pretty easy to loosen the purse strings a bit when you receive a raise. But continue budgeting as if that extra income never came along, and watch your savings grow at a higher rate. Other ways to use that bump in pay: Increase your contribution to your 401(k), individual retirement account or health savings account (remembering the maximum allowable contribution for each account).

Sign Up for Direct Deposit

Decide on a dollar amount you're willing to part with each pay period, and deposit it directly into your savings account. Without that cash immediately on hand, you're less likely to spend it. And you'll likely save more if you deposit funds up front rather than waiting to sock away whatever's left after you pay bills and buy essentials.

Consider a High-Yield Checking or Savings Account

Keep your money in an account that earns a higher interest rate as a way to build funds more quickly. Your interest earnings might not appear to be all that huge in the short term, but over time, they can add up much faster than they might in a regular savings account. Note: To qualify, you often need to maintain a minimum account balance for these higher rates, and other rules may apply.

PRO TIP

Got a raise? Instead of upgrading your lifestyle, send the extra income directly to your savings account and watch your money grow.

Try selling items you don't need or use and add that money to grow your savings.

Shop Around for Insurance

Compare your car, health and homeowners insurance rates annually to what other companies offer. If you find that another company's premium is lower for the exact same package, see if your insurance agent can match the price or negotiate a lower cost. If not, consider switching providers.

Cancel Unused Subscriptions and Memberships

If you belong to a gym, golf club or yoga studio but rarely go, start paying yourself that membership fee instead. Make a list of apps, publications and services you've subscribed to and cancel those you're not using.

Trim Your Utility Bills

Monitor your energy and water use and look for ways to cut back, like bumping up your thermostat in the summer or turning it down in the winter. A few degrees can make a noticeable difference in your savings in a year's time.

Plan Your Meals and Stick to a Shopping List

Keeping your costs down at the grocery store requires a bit of planning, but plotting your meals for the week and buying only the ingredients you need can help reduce unnecessary or impulse purchases—and you'll likely end up wasting less food. Bring along coupons and join store loyalty programs to increase your savings.

TAKING ADVANTAGE OF SENIOR DISCOUNTS

When you reach traditional retirement age, using senior discounts is an easy way to trim your spending here and there. And those small price cuts add up in the long run!

Many businesses, including movie theaters, museums, amusement parks, grocery stores, salons, state parks and even on-line services like Amazon Prime, have offers specially meant for seniors. They aren't always widely advertised—so don't be shy about asking if a senior discount is available.

Note there are sometimes restrictions involved, including discounts only given on certain days of the week or month, and policies may vary by location. Memberships to organizations like AARP can also open the door to discounts. Here, a look at a few places where it pays to be a senior.

Airfare American, Delta, Southwest, United

Clothing Stores Banana Republic, Bealls, Dressbarn, Goodwill, Kohl's, Ross Stores

Cost-Saving Membership An AARP card offers discounts on travel, shopping, dining and more.

Drugstores Walgreens, Rite-Aid

Fast Food Chains Arby's, Burger King, Jack in the Box, KFC, Long John Silver's, McDonald's, Sonic, Subway, Wendy's

Hotels Best Western, Comfort Inn, Days Inn, Holiday Inn, Marriott, Ramada, Ritz-Carlton, Westin

Restaurants Applebee's, Chili's, Denny's, IHOP, Outback Steakhouse

Getting rid of debt frees up your money for more rewarding goals.

Put Off Pricey Purchases

Do a little research when you're in the market for a big-ticket item, wait for the right time of year and buy when retailers are slashing prices. You'll find great discounts on TVs around the Super Bowl and new lawn mowers at the end of summer.

Hunt for Free or Low-Cost Entertainment

Maybe you can't go a whole year without buying expensive tickets to a theater or sporting event, but swap a few of those occasions for a picnic or a free concert, and you could save hundreds.

Sell What You're Not Using

Craigslist, eBay, Gift Card Granny and Poshmark allow unused gift cards, clothing, furniture, toys and baby gear to move on to a second life while you pocket some extra cash.

Put Yourself on a Spending Diet

Challenge yourself to go a set number of days or weeks without buying clothes or making the splurge of your choice—perhaps dining out or making any nonessential purchases. At the end of your self-imposed fast, allocate the money you would have spent to savings. ∎

113

Retirement Investing

How to plan for the future
by making smart choices today

Understanding Asset Allocation
Honing Your Recipe for Early Retirement

When it comes to saving for an early retirement, how you invest your money is just as important as how much you invest. Different asset classes—including stocks, bonds and cash equivalents—possess a range of complementary characteristics that provide investors with the ability to grow, protect and access their savings in pursuit of their long-term goals.

The strategy of balancing risk and reward by holding an appropriate mix of assets is known as asset allocation. Asset allocation uses factors such as your appetite for risk and your time frame for retirement to determine the percentage of stocks, bonds and cash that you should hold. When combined appropriately, these asset classes can provide your portfolio with the growth necessary to support your needs, while also offering protection from market downswings that can eat into your gains and could potentially delay your time line for retirement.

Because early retirees have less time to build their savings, determining an appropriate allocation is particularly critical. Consider how the main asset classes work separately and together to help you find the right mix to fit your unique circumstances.

Stocks
With the highest potential rate of return among asset classes, stocks (also known as equities) are the growth engine of your portfolio. As an asset class, equities have historically outperformed their investment counterparts. Over the past century, the S&P 500, an index of the largest U.S. equities, has had average annual returns of roughly 10 percent, while bond returns have averaged closer to 5 percent. Stocks

PRO TIP

An experienced financial adviser can help you determine the appropriate asset allocation to help you meet your goal of retiring early.

With less time to build savings, proper asset allocation is critical for early retirees.

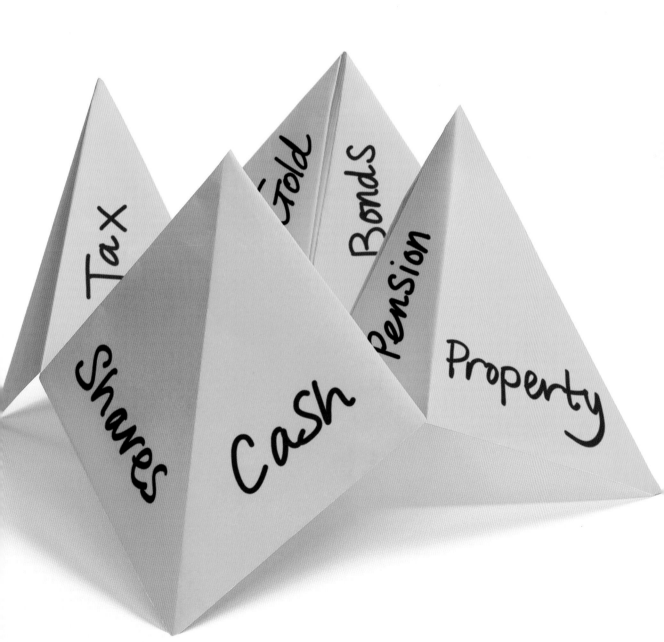

can also distribute regular payments, known as dividends, to their owners. Or they can be reinvested.

But that growth comes at a cost. While equities have the potential to generate better returns than bonds, they've also experienced more volatility, historically. The more concentrated—or heavily weighted—a portfolio is in equities, the more risk of capital losses an investor assumes.

For someone who has plenty of time before retirement to recover from potential losses, that risk can be worth it. For someone closer to quitting the grind, a significant equity allocation can be risky. That's because losses close to, or early in, retirement can take a significant bite out of a portfolio.

Sustaining losses just as you begin drawing on savings hurts the compounding potential

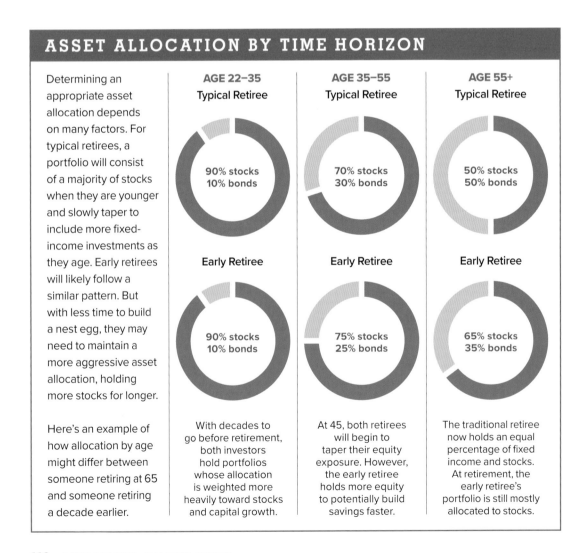

ASSET ALLOCATION BY TIME HORIZON

Determining an appropriate asset allocation depends on many factors. For typical retirees, a portfolio will consist of a majority of stocks when they are younger and slowly taper to include more fixed-income investments as they age. Early retirees will likely follow a similar pattern. But with less time to build a nest egg, they may need to maintain a more aggressive asset allocation, holding more stocks for longer.

Here's an example of how allocation by age might differ between someone retiring at 65 and someone retiring a decade earlier.

AGE 22–35
Typical Retiree

90% stocks
10% bonds

Early Retiree

90% stocks
10% bonds

With decades to go before retirement, both investors hold portfolios whose allocation is weighted more heavily toward stocks and capital growth.

AGE 35–55
Typical Retiree

70% stocks
30% bonds

Early Retiree

75% stocks
25% bonds

At 45, both retirees will begin to taper their equity exposure. However, the early retiree holds more equity to potentially build savings faster.

AGE 55+
Typical Retiree

50% stocks
50% bonds

Early Retiree

65% stocks
35% bonds

The traditional retiree now holds an equal percentage of fixed income and stocks. At retirement, the early retiree's portfolio is still mostly allocated to stocks.

of your money going forward. For that reason, many investors decide to begin tapering their exposure to equities as they near retirement. But early retirees don't always have the same luxury. With fewer years to save, they often need to maintain a more aggressive investment strategy, with a greater equity allocation.

Bonds

Bonds—or fixed income instruments—are essentially IOUs issued by a corporation or government. In buying a bond, you're effectively loaning that issuer money. In return, they promise to repay the entirety of your loan at the predetermined date, as well as regular interest payments (known as the coupon) along the way.

While bonds tend to offer less growth potential than stocks, they're also less likely to lose money during a down market. Holding a percentage of your assets in bonds can help you balance the risk in your portfolio and mitigate volatility. Coupon payments, which are determined by an agreed-upon interest rate, are more predictable than stock dividends, which vary depending upon corporate performance.

The primary risk facing bonds is rising interest rates. As rates rise, the market value of a bond you own falls. Newly issued bonds provide investors with a more competitive yield, making older ones less attractive, and thus less valuable.

Cash

The advantage of cash and cash equivalents—which include certificates of deposit (CDs) and money market accounts—over both stocks and bonds is their liquidity. Cash is directly redeemable for goods and services. Stocks and bonds must be sold or liquidated for cash, a process that can take days, in some cases. So

Diversify your investments to offset the risk of volatility.

to meet emergencies and short-term spending needs, cash is king.

Cash is also the safest investment in a portfolio. Without exposure to interest rates or the movements of the stock market, cash isn't subject to the same risks as equities or bonds. But cash isn't entirely devoid of risk, as inflation can sap the buying power of your cash investments.

Understanding asset allocation is key to developing an investment strategy that effectively balances risk and return. As you approach an early retirement it's important to carefully evaluate that allocation, considering how well it serves your current needs and how it will shift over time to help you reach them going forward. ■

**Don't put all your eggs—or
your money—in one basket.**

The Importance of a Diversified Portfolio
Spreading Out Your Risk to Protect Your Savings

I nvesting always brings with it some degree of risk. After all, you can't control fluctuations in the market or losses in a particular stock or sector. But by spreading your investments across different types of assets, you can mitigate the impact of potential losses and reduce your portfolio's overall volatility. This strategy is known as diversification.

Diversification is a smart move for most investors, but if you're planning for an early retirement, it can be especially beneficial. As you move into retirement, you are likely to start relying more on investments to help cover basic expenses, and volatility in your portfolio can be more consequential. For example, while you're earning income from work, a down year for your portfolio may not affect you much—and you can afford to wait for it to get back on track. In retirement, however, you may not have that luxury if you have no outside income and are forced to draw from your investments The particular mix of investments you hold will depend on your current financial situation, risk tolerance and time horizon. Try incorporating these strategies to diversify your portfolio and mitigate risk.

Diversification Among Asset Classes
Diversification starts with allocating your investments across broad categories of assets. For example, stocks have high growth potential and relatively high risk levels, while bonds have lower growth potential and come with less risk. Just as importantly, stocks and bonds don't necessarily respond to the same economic triggers. An event that sends equity markets plunging may have little effect on the bond market, while soaring stocks may coincide with relatively stagnant bond performance. Declines in one asset class can be softened or offset by gains in another asset class.

Moving beyond the world of stocks and bonds may further reduce volatility by introducing a greater array of noncorrelated investments to your portfolio. Nontraditional investments such

121

Stocks, bonds and real estate can all play a role in a diversified portfolio.

happen that harmed the entire industry, your portfolio would take a big hit. Investing across different industries and sectors provides protection against this sort of damage.

Likewise, investing in companies of various sizes can add a layer of risk protection, since large-cap, mid-cap and small-cap stocks may perform differently in the same year. Region is another variable. In particular, adding exposure to international investments may help you weather downturns in domestic markets. Even within bonds, diversification is possible: High-yield bonds don't correlate perfectly with investment-grade corporate bonds, and global bonds behave differently than domestic bonds.

Diversifying With Mutual Funds

If selecting the perfect mix of investments sounds intimidating, mutual funds can be a good resource. Mutual funds allow you to pool your money with other investors in a collective fund that is invested in a preselected mix of assets. Most mutual funds hold more than 100 securities, giving them a level of diversification that would be difficult, if not impossible, to achieve for most individual investors. Mutual funds may be managed actively or passively. (See "Active vs. Passive Funds," opposite page.)

Mutual funds can include not just stocks but bonds, commodities and other assets. In this respect, they can offer an entry point into less-familiar investments, providing an opportunity for a higher level of diversification.

Balancing Growth Potential and Risk

As you approach, and enter into, retirement, you'll probably want to shift your portfolio to a more conservative mix of investments. But it's important to hold on to some assets with higher

as real estate, commodities and private equity come with certain risks, but when managed judiciously can play a part in a well-diversified retirement strategy.

Diversification Within Asset Classes

Diversification becomes even more powerful when applied within asset classes. Say you invest in a single stock, like a technology company. Your investment success is directly tied to the performance of this one company. If you invest in two technology companies, you're slightly better diversified, and the success of one may help you weather a rough period for the other.

But sometimes there are economic events that affect entire sectors. If all your investments were in tech companies and something were to growth potential. This is especially true if you're planning to retire early, since you should expect a longer retirement than traditional retirees. Exposure to higher-risk, higher-reward stocks can help you keep up with inflation and provide the growth you need for a decades-long retirement.

Diversification doesn't eliminate the risks that come with such investments. Instead, it provides protection against potential downturns by including assets that continue to grow while other assets may be declining. The further your portfolio sinks in a downturn, the longer it may take to recover. A well-diversified mix of stocks, bonds and other assets can keep your portfolio from sinking too low and help you maintain a steady income for as long as your retirement lasts. ■

ACTIVE VS. PASSIVE FUNDS

Mutual funds are typically managed in one of two ways. Actively managed funds are overseen by a professional portfolio manager (or a team of managers) who aim to beat the performance of a benchmark index by actively selecting securities to invest in. Passively managed funds, on the other hand, are constructed to track the performance of a specific index.

Active Funds

Active funds come with all the benefits and drawbacks of a more hands-on management style. They usually charge higher fees, but you gain the expertise of a knowledgeable professional investor who is working to maximize your short- and long-term growth. Managers of active funds analyze broad trends, economic sectors and individual assets to make educated guesses about future performance.

Managed well, an active fund can provide higher returns than a fund that's mostly left to its own devices. The risk is that the manager will guess wrong more often than right—in which case, an active fund may perform worse than a passive fund. In fact, this happens with most actively managed funds: As of December 2017, more than 84 percent of large-cap funds had underperformed the S&P 500 over the past five years, according to S&P Dow Jones Indices. There is also a higher likelihood that an active fund will bring returns that trigger a capital gains tax.

Between the fees, the taxes and the risk that an active fund will underperform market indexes, many investors would be better off investing in low-cost, passively managed index funds.

Passive Funds

Passively managed index funds are tied to major indexes, like the S&P 500 or the Dow Jones Industrial Average. They provide exposure to a wide array of securities while harnessing the long-term growth potential of markets on a broad scale. When an index gains or loses a particular security, the index fund automatically readjusts to reflect the new mix of assets.

Passive funds typically have very low fees, since they don't require much labor on a manager's part. They also offer high levels of transparency, so you always know exactly which assets you're investing in. And if you hold them in a taxable investment account, they come with a low risk of triggering capital gains taxes, since there is typically little turnover among the underlying funds.

The Role of Rebalancing
Stay on Track by Adjusting Your Investments

**Read your statements
so you can determine
how your investments
are performing.**

When you first invested, you may have crafted the perfect mix of stocks, bonds and cash based on your age, goals, financial situation and risk tolerance. But as the years go by and the markets fluctuate, that mix will naturally be pulled out of balance. For example, while the past few years have been good to stock investors, rising values may have tilted your portfolio too heavily toward stocks. A portfolio that's too stock-heavy could expose you to more risk than you are actually prepared for.

The good news: You can correct this situation with regular rebalancing. Here's a look at how rebalancing works—and when and how you should do it.

What Is Rebalancing?

Rebalancing your portfolio gives you a chance to review and reassess your investments. This process allows you to see which investments are

All portfolios need rebalancing over time as the markets shift.

doing well and what's not working. When you rebalance, if you notice an investment that's not meeting your goals or is otherwise problematic, you can take this opportunity to make a change.

Rebalancing also offers an opportunity to be sure that your asset allocation reflects your intentions. For example, after a great year in the market, you may find your stocks are taking up a bigger portion of your portfolio than you'd planned. While those stocks may be seeing great returns, they may also open you up to risk. Because stocks tend to be more volatile than other types of investments, portfolios with a greater percentage of stocks will see more extreme ups and downs than portfolios with a smaller proportion of stocks. Your portfolio mix should take into consideration how much risk you can handle and your individual investment strategy. In this scenario, rebalancing your portfolio away from stocks can help make sure that you're not taking on too much risk.

Keep in mind that dividing your investments among varying asset classes is not the only requirement for maintaining a balanced portfolio. You should also aim to diversify your investments within each asset class. For instance, you might spread your stock holdings among companies of various sizes, sectors and locations. You can diversify bond holdings across sector, maturity, credit quality and geography. As the economy and business cycles evolve, various investments and markets will perform differently. A diverse portfolio minimizes the risk that any one investment or sector will pull down your whole portfolio and undermine your ability to reach your financial goals.

PRO TIP

Plan to review your allocation once or twice each year, plus any time you experience a major life change, like a birth or job change.

When to Rebalance

Set a regular time frame in which to review your investments, such as once or twice a year. An annual review is a good minimum amount of time to do an analysis, with additional check-ins following any big life changes such as a job change, a major move, the birth of a child or a death in the family.

Alternatively, you might decide to rebalance whenever your portfolio is out of balance by a certain amount. If you choose to follow this strategy, you might assess your portfolio when your mix of investments fluctuates away from your target allocation by 5 percentage points, for example.

Reviewing Your Investments

A thorough rebalancing process offers an opportunity to review your portfolio as a whole. When it's time to rebalance, start by reviewing your mutual fund holdings, determining how each fund has performed compared to its benchmark (an index listed in the fund's prospectus). By design, of course, low-cost index funds will track their underlying index very closely, while actively managed mutual funds aim to beat the performance of their benchmark index. If you hold actively managed funds, it's worth checking out documents such as annual reports and other filings that will tell you about big changes. Keep an eye out for any major shifts, such as new investment strategies, a new portfolio manager or fee increases.

If you hold individual stocks or bonds, review them as well. Consider past performance and future outlook, as well as whether they represent an appropriate portion of your portfolio. As a general rule, you may want to avoid having a single security represent more than 10 percent of your portfolio's value.

As you're assessing your holdings, bear in mind that the key to successful investing is assembling a well-diversified portfolio and holding it for the long term. If you're confident in your initial plan, there is no need to buy and sell securities frequently—and doing so can even harm your prospects, as humans are notoriously bad at predicting market performance.

How to Rebalance

After you've reviewed your investments, it's time to make any changes that are necessary to bring your portfolio in line with your plan. The quickest method of correcting imbalances is to sell one type of your investments in order to buy another one. For instance, say your target asset allocation is 60 percent stocks and 40 percent bonds. As a result of the long bull market, stocks now represent 70 percent of your holdings. You might decide to sell enough of your stock holdings to get back to your target allocation, and use the proceeds to buy an equivalent amount of bonds.

If you're comfortable rebalancing at a slower pace, you can use new contributions to correct imbalances. In the scenario above, you could direct all new contributions to your bond funds. Over time, the balance of your holdings would gradually shift back toward your target.

Readjusting the balance of your portfolio as needed can help minimize risk and keep your investment portfolio healthy. If you remain disciplined about rebalancing, even when markets are doing well and you're pleased with your returns, you'll ensure you're staying on track with your investment plan over time. ∎

Rebalancing keeps your portfolio from taking on too much— or not enough—risk.

06 | **INVEST REGULARLY** | 01 | 02 | 03 | 04 | 05 | 06

The Importance of Investing Regularly
Using Dollar-Cost Averaging
to Ride the Waves of the Markets

Investing can feel exciting, overwhelming or stressful. Whatever the case may be, you might be eager to toss a large sum into the market all at once and hope you've timed it right.

But the smarter strategy is to invest your money consistently over time. Regular investments are part of a strategy known as dollar-cost averaging, which typically involves investing a fixed dollar amount on a monthly or biweekly basis. If you have a 401(k) account, you're already practicing dollar-cost averaging, as your contributions are automatically invested every pay period.

It's hard—if not impossible—to predict what's going to happen in the market, and trying to do so can lead you to make costly mistakes. By investing at regular intervals, you'll sometimes buy when prices are higher and sometimes when they're lower. The set dollar amount you're investing buys fewer shares when prices are up and more shares when they're down, ultimately reducing the average cost of your shares.

The advantage to dollar-cost averaging is that you don't have to worry about the timing of your investment. Over time, the market peaks and valleys average out. And the gains on shares you snag when prices are low can make up for the shares you paid more for when prices were high.

This method also ensures that on at least some of the days you're investing, the market will be down—a time when some investors are selling out of fear and others might be afraid to buy. After a downturn, the market tends to go up, so buying at these moments while prices are low can help you secure gains in the long run. ■

PRO TIP

Rather than trying to time the market, invest on a regular schedule. This strategy, over time, smooths out the peaks and valleys of the markets.

Making regular 401(k) contributions is one example of dollar-cost averaging.

Keep an Eye on Investing Costs
Don't Let Fees and Other Expenses Eat Up Your Profits

The savvy investor knows that investing isn't free. The fees and management costs of investing can add up quickly, so it helps to be aware of them and know what to expect. Stay on the lookout for these investment fees and costs.

Mutual-Fund Management Fees

Nearly all mutual funds charge annual fees, but how much you'll actually pay can vary. The costs often depend on whether the fund is actively or passively managed. Actively managed funds usually have higher fees, as they're run by experienced professionals who are pursuing a specific investment strategy that may require specialized knowledge. On the other hand, passively managed funds use computer models to try to replicate the performance of a particular index, and their fees are typically lower as a result. Other fund charges might cover services such as marketing and accounting.

What you'll pay for these services should be disclosed in the fund's prospectus; look for the fund's expense ratio. (You can also usually find this information in your brokerage account's online portal.) But be aware that the expense ratio may not include some costs, such as sales charges and redemption fees. Pay close attention to how much of your returns will go toward fees when selecting which fund is the right one for you.

Commissions

Trading frequently can cost you a lot in commission fees. These fees vary greatly from firm to firm. You can reduce these costs by using commission-free exchange-traded funds or no-load mutual funds. Also, consider limiting your trading to only occasional rebalancing.

PRO TIP

When researching a mutual fund, check the fund's expense ratio and compare it to other similar funds before you buy shares.

Check a fund's prospectus or your brokerage account's online portal for fees.

Taxes on Capital Gains

Buying and selling too often may mean that you end up owing more in capital gains taxes (assuming you're making these trades in a taxable account rather than in a tax-deferred retirement account). The term "short-term capital gains" refer to profits on investments that have been held for less than a year, and which are thereby taxed at normal income tax rates. Long-term capital gains are taxed at a much lower rate of 15 percent or 20 percent, depending on what your tax bracket may be. Maintaining a buy-and-hold strategy can help you avoid paying more in taxes.

Brokerage Fees

Depending on your broker, you may find yourself on the hook for a laundry list of small fees—such as those for paper statements, annual fees and inactivity fees—that can add up. You may be able to eliminate some of these, like a monthly fee for paper statements, by receiving statements online. But if you don't plan to trade often and incur hundreds of dollars in fees for inactivity, you may want to research another brokerage firm.

Some investment costs are unavoidable; others may be worth the price. Working to reduce costs can make a big difference on your returns. ∎

If looking at your account balances too often stresses you out, take a break.

Don't Let Emotion Rule Your Strategy
Remain Levelheaded and Keep Investing

The ups and downs of volatile markets can make investing an unpredictable, and at times harrowing, experience. During these market swings, it's only human to feel emotional, and it can be tempting to let those emotions rule your reactions. For example, during a bull market, you may see risky investments doing well and feel the urge to purchase securities that don't match your current investment strategy. Conversely, when the market is doing poorly, you may be tempted to sell off your stock.

Your financial plan should already account for your risk tolerance as well as market volatility. To follow either of the above impulses puts your financial plan in jeopardy.

Consider the following ways to keep your emotions in check.

Understand the Downside of Emotional Investing

An awareness of emotions and the role they play in decision making is key for any investor. People are naturally averse to loss and may overreact in an effort to prevent it. Preserving your wealth, however, requires looking ahead and not making rash moves based on how a loss—or potential loss—feels in the moment.

If you follow your impulses, the decisions you make out of fear or excitement may soon backfire. Even when people know better, they often focus more on short-term outcomes than the long-term consequences. And most do a poor job of predicting how a decision today will affect the future.

Acting on your gut reactions can lead you to make choices that go against your investment strategy. For instance, when the stock market is doing well, good returns might entice you to take on too much stock, which could throw your portfolio out of balance. Likewise, a roaring stock market can tempt you to pour extra

---

PRO TIP

If market fluctuations throw you into a nail-biting frenzy, take a look at historical market patterns to keep things in perspective.

133

cash into seemingly can't-miss companies. But buying at the market's peak could mean your investments have nowhere to go but down.

What's more, giving in to the urge to sell your stocks when they've lost value means you could lock in your losses and miss out on the eventual recovery when it happens later—and history shows that markets will, eventually, recover their losses.

Avoid Emotional Investing

To avoid allowing your emotions to dictate your financial decisions, consider the following strategies:

Stay Focused on Your Long-Term Goals Your financial plan has taken volatility into account, but if you tinker with your mix of investments because of emotion, you can throw that plan out of whack. Major market news or even big events outside the market can inspire strong feelings and have you itching to change up your investments. When you feel pressured to buy or sell, stick to the plan.

Don't Track Returns Too Closely In the short term, market volatility can seem amplified, but the roller coaster is likely to feel less dramatic over time. Don't watch the market closely and you're less likely to notice a bumpy ride. So stay away from cable news and consider deleting market updates from your phone.

Be Aware of Your Feelings If you're feeling stressed from a conflict in your personal life or some large-scale drama you're following in the news, know that the stress might affect your ability to make sound financial decisions. Remind yourself to take a breather before you act. It's also useful to be aware of emotional patterns, such as indecisiveness, fear or comparing another investor's success to your own. Pay attention to these feelings so you can take a step back and reconsider their role in your decision-making process.

Look to History Taking a long look in the rearview mirror can sometimes help put things in perspective. When you consider market declines of the past, you'll also see how markets recovered. Those who remain invested during downturns are often able to take advantage of subsequent recoveries. This view might help make current downturns feel a little less dire.

Have a Buy-and-Sell Strategy Instead of making moves on a whim, use strategies like buying low and selling high. A rules-based approach to investing can keep the emotional component out of your decisions.

Prioritize Diversification Different asset classes respond in different ways to market shifts. If you diversify across asset classes, you can avoid feeling the full brunt of market movements.

Follow an Expert's Advice A financial adviser can help you analyze the market and make well-reasoned moves with your money. Bounce ideas off your adviser when you're feeling particularly worried or excited about an investment. Remember: You can always lean on the advice of someone with both expertise and emotional distance.

It can be challenging to push your emotions to the side and let a coolheaded, rational approach decide your next move. You're human, so feeling swayed by emotion is only natural. But smart investing considers the way emotion can influence decisions and tries to dial it down. Make financial decisions with a careful, deliberate strategy—and stick to it for long-term success. ■

Markets will rise and fall; tune out the noise and keep investing.

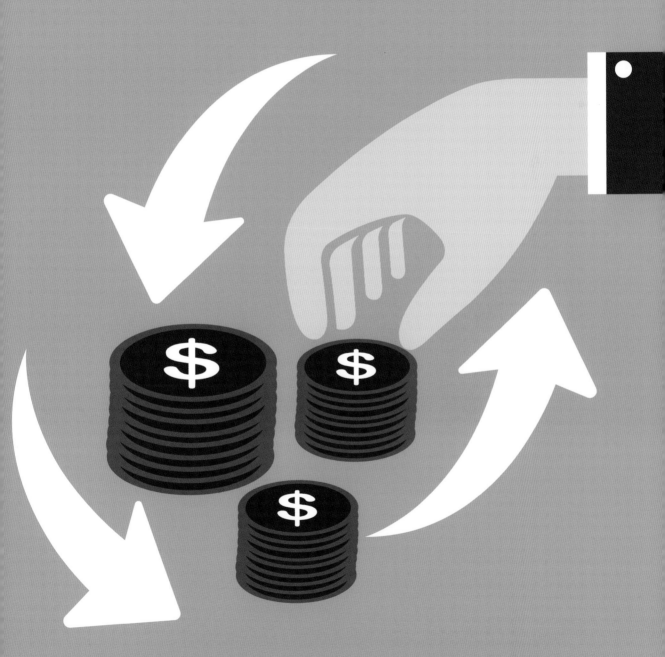

Plan for Retirement Income

Creating a strategy for making your money work

07 INFLATION 01 | 02 | 03 | 04 | 05 | 06 | 07 | 08

Preparing for Inflation
Protecting Your Nest Egg From Rising Costs

As you nail down your goals and invest for the future, you'll want to consider the effects of inflation on your savings. A certain amount of inflation is expected: The Federal Reserve aims to keep the inflation rate to about 2 percent a year. However, economies also experience unexpected inflation, which can have a big impact on your retirement savings. Knowing that the cost of goods and services will rise over time, you'll need your retirement income to rise, too.

Find a balance between growth and preservation with a combination of stocks, inflation-protected investments and accounts that pay an interest rate at or above the rate of inflation. Consider these three strategies when preparing for inflation in retirement.

Stay Invested

To help beat inflation, it's smart to stay invested in stocks and stock mutual funds. The average annual return of the S&P 500 is roughly 10 percent, more than outstripping the historical annual inflation rate of about 3 percent. The longer you can stay in the stock market, the longer you can take advantage of these potential returns. A moderate plan may include 40 to 60 percent in stocks at the start of retirement, with the rest in cash and fixed-income investments to balance out risk.

Of course, timing is everything with the stock market. You'll want to work with a financial adviser to determine what mix of assets works best for you now and as you get older, given your early-retirement plans.

Consider Inflation-Protected Products

Inflation-protected products are built with the ability to keep pace with inflation. One common inflation-protected tool is a fixed annuity with a cost of living adjustment, or COLA, rider. Fixed annuities allow you to pay a premium and receive a guaranteed amount of income each

Keep your money growing, to meet rising costs over time.

139

There are many different ways to hedge against inflation over time.

month starting at a specific point in time. Fixed annuities guarantee the principal investment plus a fixed-interest rate. The COLA rider keeps annuity income on pace with inflation.

Another option is Treasury inflation-protected securities (TIPS), low-risk, government-backed bonds that accrue semiannual inflation adjustments plus fixed coupon—or interest—rates. This means that the principal will be adjusted according to the inflation rate, and the interest rate will be added to the new principal. When it comes time to collect the return, the investor receives an amount equal to either the original principal they invested or an adjusted higher principal due to inflation. The original principal is never-lost—as long as the bond is held for the length of the contract. TIPS are also exempt from state and local taxes, allowing you to keep more of the money when you do decide to collect the return.

> **PRO TIP**
>
> Consider investing in Treasury inflation-protected securities (TIPS), government-backed bonds designed to protect against inflation.

Consider Renting Out Your Property

Until the pandemic brought the U.S. real estate market to a temporary halt, many local markets were growing—and they're expected to continue their long-term growth before long. That means housing is in high demand and rent prices reflect local inflation. If you own property in a desirable location, you should have no issues finding tenants who are willing to pay higher prices for your rental. Take the town of Bozeman, Montana, for example. Because of the influx of new residents, housing prices have increased more than 55 percent since 2012. If you live in an area like this, where rents are increasing, you may think about leasing a room in—or all of—your house to capitalize on the demand. (Do bear in mind the logistical challenges, costs and local regulations.) Collecting rent checks might not make you rich, but it can give you another source of income to add to your revenue stream.

Staying active in your investing can help you protect yourself from the effects of inflation so you can be sure to meet your cash flow needs as you near retirement. ∎

The cost of goods and services rises; your retirement income needs to rise, too.

A part-time job
could provide
many benefits.

Working in Retirement
A Part-Time Job Offers
Financial and Social Benefits

Retiring early—or even on time—may not actually look like traditional retirement for many people. Increases in longevity mean that people who plan to retire at 65 should plan for at least 30 years of retirement. If you're retiring ahead of that schedule, that number can grow even higher.

This shift has two major implications for how you might think about work after retirement. First, 30 or 40 years (or more!) is an awfully long time to spend simply pursuing your hobbies and reading novels—potentially missing the fulfillment and social engagement that work can provide. Second, you're going to have to foot the bill for a series of expenses over that time, and it may be challenging to save all of it by the time you hit your early-retirement goal. That's why it's worth considering continuing to work for some time after you've retired from your career.

If you choose to keep working or return to work, you don't have to stick with the same full-time role you had previously. Depending on the flexibility of your employer, your schedule could be much more relaxed, or your workload lighter. Or you might consider a self-employed gig in which you set your own hours and terms, or even take on a part-time job in an industry that's completely new to you.

No matter which approach you take, getting several more years of income under your belt can provide a big payoff—keeping you satisfied, connected and well-funded for many years to come. Here are a few of the advantages that working after retirement can provide:

Postpone Drawing on Your Investments
Working another job may not be what you had in mind for your days postretirement. But earning

> **PRO TIP**
>
> Delay claiming Social Security benefits as long as possible, so your monthly Social Security checks will be larger down the road.

Studies show that staying socially active can improve health.

a little extra cash might allow you to delay drawing down your investment portfolio's principal.

Not only does this preserve your principal for later years—it also allows your investments to grow and provides more opportunities for you to add to your savings, which could leave you with a bigger nest egg.

Get the Tax Advantages

If you work during your retirement and are able to delay relying on your savings, you may earn enough to keep contributing to tax-advantaged 401(k) and IRA plans. Traditional IRAs don't allow contributions past age 70½, but you can contribute to a Roth IRA as long as you have earned income—no matter your age.

Allowing your tax-advantaged investments to grow while you rely on other sources of income can have major results. Imagine you can avoid taking $15,000 from your IRA withdrawals for 10 years and that the funds continue growing, tax-deferred, at an annualized rate of 8 percent. After 10 years, you'd have $220,000 more than you would have if you'd continued making those $15,000 withdrawals.

Collect Bigger Social Security Checks

Working longer might also allow you to delay claiming Social Security checks. The longer you're able to put off receiving Social Security payments (until age 70), the larger your checks will be when you do start collecting. If you can continue working, you'll get the benefit of seeing a boost to your Social Security down the road.

If you're already collecting Social Security and take a job in retirement, keep in mind that your new source of income might affect how much you receive in your monthly government checks.

Consider Your Health Needs

If you're under 65 and not yet eligible for Medicare, you may want to remain covered by health benefits through an employer. In this case, you might want to look for a job that provides these benefits instead of shelling out money to cover premiums and medical bills completely on your own. And don't assume you need to go back to full-time work: Retailers including Costco, Whole Foods and Starbucks, among others, offer health insurance benefits for part-timers.

Keeping a job in retirement can support your financial health—and it may also have emotional and psychological benefits. Without those business lunches, meetings with colleagues and clients and small talk over coffee in the break room, retirement can be an isolating experience.

And it turns out that social engagement isn't just nice to have—it has tangible benefits. In fact, a study by the Rush Alzheimer's Disease Center found that seniors who are highly social have a 70 percent lower rate of cognitive decline than their less social peers. And isolation among older adults is linked to worse physical and mental health, which means maintaining social connections is especially beneficial in retirement. Picking up even part-time work could help stave off feelings of loneliness and boredom, and provide the engagement you need to stay healthy.

The benefits to working in retirement could be profound, both personally and financially. Postpone full retirement for several years—or dip in and out of paid work over the years—and you may see a big impact on both your financial stability and your overall fulfillment. ∎

PRO TIP

Landing a part-time job with health insurance can allow early retirees access to affordable health care until they're eligible for Medicare.

07 | **ANNUITIES** | 01 | 02 | 03 | 04 | 05 | 06 | 07 | 08

Could an Annuity Be Right for You?
Using the Investment to Provide a Predictable Income Stream

With so much uncertainty surrounding retirement, many people want a dependable source of income that they can rely on to cover basic expenses. Annuities guarantee a steady income stream, month after month, for many years. As part of a comprehensive retirement strategy, they can give you the peace of mind that comes with predictable payments.

If you're planning an early retirement and have maxed out your retirement savings plans, annuities can be an excellent place to invest additional savings. They offer many of the same tax benefits as IRAs and 401(k)s—but without the contribution limits.

That being said, annuities aren't right for everyone. They are relatively inflexible investment options and sometimes carry onerous fees. To find out if an annuity fits with your retirement plan, consider the different options available and weigh their advantages and drawbacks.

Immediate vs. Deferred Annuities

When you purchase an annuity, you make an investment that begins paying out sometime in the future. You can receive income from an annuity on a monthly, quarterly or annual basis. Note that withdrawals made before age 59½ may be subject to a 10 percent penalty, in addition to being taxed as income.

Immediate annuities start paying out right after you make your initial investment, while deferred annuities allow withdrawals beginning at a pre-selected later date. Immediate annuities may make sense for people who are at or nearing their official retirement age. If you're planning to retire early but are still several years from your target retirement age, a deferred annuity is probably preferable.

Fixed-Rate vs. Variable Annuities

You can also choose between fixed-rate and variable annuities. Fixed-rate annuities have predetermined payouts that provide more

Annuities vary in terms of payout options, rates and fees.

certainty, while the more flexible variable annuity payments are tied to the performance of an investment portfolio. Fixed-rate annuities provide more certainty about payouts, while variable annuities offer more flexibility and growth opportunity.

With variable annuities, you can decide which investment vehicles your money goes into. They often offer a guaranteed minimum payment, and their higher growth potential gives them a better chance at keeping up with inflation. On the other hand, since they are more actively managed, they typically are associated with higher expenses.

Payout Options

When you purchase an annuity, you decide not only when to start collecting payouts, but how long those payouts will last and whether your heirs stand to benefit from the investment.

One option is to collect payments for a set number of years, granting the remaining payments to a beneficiary if you die during that period. Another option is to collect payments for the duration of your life, the amount of which is determined by how much you invest and your life expectancy. If you choose the lifetime payment option, you can also designate a beneficiary to continue to receive payouts if you die during a specified period.

Different types of annuities offer other benefits. A joint and

PRO TIP

If you're browsing annuities, be sure you fully understand the associated fees, commissions and any withdrawal penalties you might face.

Factor in the benefits and risks of different annuity plans.

survivor annuity guarantees that in the case of your death, your beneficiary will receive payouts for the rest of his or her life. A charitable gift annuity allows you to donate to the charity of your choice while receiving a fixed income stream for the rest of your life.

No matter which type of annuity you choose, the money in it grows tax-deferred. When you start taking withdrawals, only the earnings are taxed as income; the amount you originally contributed can be withdrawn tax-free.

Caveats

One drawback to annuities is that they can come with an array of fees. If you're not careful, the gains on your annuity investment can be offset by these expenses. Variable annuities often charge high annual fees, including insurance charges, management fees and fees for various riders. Additionally, some annuities are sold by insurance brokers who collect a commission that can be as high as 10 percent. And if you withdraw money from your annuity prematurely—typically in the first several years after you buy it—you may face a surrender charge of anywhere from 5 to 20 percent. That's in addition to the 10 percent penalty you'll be hit with if you start taking withdrawals before age 59½.

While you should be aware that these expenses exist, there are also inexpensive annuity options that won't penalize you with hefty fees. Research all annuities thoroughly and ask your financial adviser about hidden costs.

Are annuities right for you? That all depends on how close you are to retirement, how much you have invested elsewhere and your overall risk tolerance. If having a predictable income stream is important to you, an annuity can be an excellent complement to Social Security, 401(k)s, IRAs, brokerage accounts and other investments in your portfolio. ∎

Awaiting a Pension
What You Need to Know About Your Plan

These days, many people build their careers by moving from business to business, holding multiple jobs before settling in to a long-term role. However, if you are lucky enough to have enjoyed a long career with one company, you may be rewarded with a pension as part of your retirement income. Although private-sector pensions are on the decline, many fields in the public sector—including education, health care, government and the military—are still offering pension plans for their employees.

Pensions provide guaranteed income through your retirement, and it's important to figure out how early retirement can affect your plan. If you're a nurse or teacher and your pension kicks in after a certain number of years on the job, you could be ready to retire and receive your pension at age 55. On the other hand, retiring early might mean you won't receive as much money, or that you're excluded from the pension plan altogether.

Pensions are more rare than they once were, but they're still common in the public sector.

149

Plan for your pension to be taxed as ordinary income and be aware that some employers can impose a clawback—a legal provision that allows them to retroactively reduce pension payments and take back money that's already been disbursed to you.

If you're planning to receive a pension, here's what you'll want to know about fitting it into your retirement plan.

Pension Types

Most pension plans pay recipients a set annual income in retirement, regardless of the performance of the underlying investments. The formula for this amount varies, but it's typically based on age, salary and the number of years you worked for the company. If the underlying investment portfolio doesn't produce returns sufficient to pay out the pension amount, the employer must make up the difference—meaning that pensions offer a level of security that 401(k) plans do not.

Vesting Schedules

If your company practices cliff vesting, you'll have to stay with the company for a designated period of time to earn your pension. For example, if the threshold is five years and you leave the company before your five-year anniversary, you'll receive no pension at all. But if you stay past five years, you're eligible for 100 percent of your promised benefit.

Graded vesting, or partial vesting, allows employees to become vested over time. Let's say you leave the job after your second year and

PRO TIP

If you have access to a vested pension plan, consider working until you're 100 percent vested to maximize your retirement income.

you're entitled to 20 percent of your benefit. For each subsequent year you work for the company, you qualify for another 10 percent. The schedule continues until you reach your 10th year, when you're 100 percent vested.

Payment Options

When it comes time to collect your pension, you can typically choose between a lump-sum payout and a monthly payment. Many

A pension can provide a predictable source of retirement income.

retirees choose a monthly payout, in the form of an annuity that provides a steady stream of income for the rest of your life. Combined with other forms of retirement income, monthly pension payments can help you meet your cash-flow needs over time.

Still, some experienced investors prefer one large payout so they can invest the funds on their own. Receiving a lump sum allows you to turn around and reinvest the money, then manage your own monthly allowances as needed. Of course, this approach means that the recipients assume full responsibility for their money and will have to be smart about making it last.

If you're fortunate enough to have a pension, it pays to know how it works—when you can access it, how much it will be and whether the timing of your retirement will affect it. Consider consulting a financial adviser to determine which payout option best suits your needs. ∎

The size of your Social Security benefits is based on your top 35 years of income.

Social Security Claiming Strategies
Making the Most of Your Benefits

Social Security is one of the forms of guaranteed income that you will be able to claim in retirement. For most people, the earliest you can begin collecting benefits is age 62. For someone aiming for early retirement, that may seem a long way away, but it's worth taking a little time now to understand how to maximize your future benefits.

The amount of money you'll receive from Social Security is calculated based on your top 35 years of earned income, and it varies depending on when you decide to start claiming Social Security. Below are some strategies to consider to help you make the most of your Social Security benefits.

It Pays to Delay

It can be very tempting to tap into your Social Security benefits as soon as you're eligible for them at age 62. However, doing so likely means forgoing a larger benefit later.

Social Security determines "full retirement age" (FRA) as somewhere between age 65 and 67, depending on the year you were born. Tapping into your benefits before FRA means a reduction in benefits, which can be substantial. For each year that you delay benefits between the ages of 62 and 70, you could see as much as an 8 percent increase in benefits. Once you reach age 70, there's no advantage to waiting longer to claim. But if you can create a strategy to cover your expenses with other income streams as long as possible up to age 70, it may well be worth the wait.

Claiming Strategies for Couples

For married couples, deciding when each spouse should begin claiming Social Security can be a nuanced process. Factors to consider include any age difference between the spouses, which spouse was

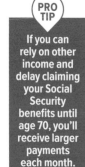

PRO TIP

If you can rely on other income and delay claiming your Social Security benefits until age 70, you'll receive larger payments each month.

Delaying benefits now saves money down the road.

the higher earner and whether one spouse has a limited work history.

Members of a couple can choose between taking their own benefit or taking a spousal benefit of up to 50 percent of their spouse's benefit. For couples in which one person was a much higher earner, taking the spousal benefit in lieu of one's own benefit can be advantageous.

In families in which one spouse earned significantly more, the lower-earning spouse may choose to start claiming his or her benefits at full retirement age, then switch to the spousal benefit once the other member of the couple has reached full retirement age. For example, say a lower-earning spouse's benefits at FRA are $1,000 per month, and he is three years younger than his wife, whose benefits at full retirement age will be $2,500. The lower-earning spouse could elect to receive his own benefits of $1,000 per month until his wife starts collecting her benefits at her full retirement age. At that point, he could switch to the higher spousal benefit of $1,250 per month.

UNDERSTANDING FULL RETIREMENT AGE

While you can begin claiming Social Security once you reach age 62, the age when you become eligible to receive your full Social Security benefits without reductions hovers between 65 and 67. The exact age is dependent on the year in which you were born. Consider the following birth years (based on the year 2020).

Prior to 1938 Your full retirement age is 65.

Between 1938 and 1942 You have a full retirement age of 65 plus two months added

each year. For example, if you were born in 1938, your full retirement age would be 65 and two months; for those born in 1939, it would be 65 and four months, and so on.

Between 1943 and 1954 Your full retirement age is 66.

From 1955 through 1959 You have a full retirement age of 66 plus two months added for each year after 1955.

1960 and later Your full retirement age is 67.

If at all possible, the higher-earning spouse should consider delay claiming until age 70 to take advantage of the increased benefits mentioned earlier. Besides increasing the monthly Social Security benefit, this approach also increases benefits for the surviving spouse. When one member of the couple dies, the surviving spouse can elect to receive the deceased spouse's full Social Security income as a survivor benefit in lieu of his or her own benefit. If the higher-earning spouse dies first, this provision can create a valuable source of income for the survivor.

How Income From a Job
Can Affect Your Benefits

A part-time job or side hustle can help you stay afloat financially in early retirement. But if you begin claiming Social Security before FRA, that income could mean a reduction in benefit. In this scenario—you haven't reached full retirement age and you're still earning income—Social Security will deduct $1 from your benefit payments for each $2 you earn over a set amount ($18,240 in 2020; visit ssa.gov for the up-to-date figures).

On the other hand, if you can wait until at least full retirement age to begin claiming, working a part-time job in early retirement can potentially increase your benefit: If you haven't yet accumulated 35 years of work history, working for a few more years means that you'll have more earnings from which Social Security will calculate your benefit.

Whether you can wait to take Social Security benefits will depend on your financial situation, but if you can, it may truly pay off. ∎

Sensible Withdrawal Strategies
Deciding on an Approach That Works for You

For more than two decades, one of the most talked-about ideas in retirement planning has been the so-called 4 percent rule. Devised by financial planner William Bengen as part of a 1994 study, the elegant rule was backed up by plenty of data. Bengen compared various withdrawal patterns against historical market returns going back to 1926. He found that a 4 percent withdrawal of one's starting balance, adjusted each year for inflation, was the largest withdrawal retirees could make while maintaining a steady shot at keeping their finances afloat for 30 years.

But current trends—like increasing life expectancy—cast doubt on whether the 4 percent rule is the best way to keep from outliving your income during a long retirement. For early retirees, the possibility of running out of assets is an even greater concern, given that they may live longer on top of starting their retirement earlier.

Though it's still worth understanding the 4 percent rule, it's also important to consider other income withdrawal strategies.

The 4 Percent Rule Explained

The 4 percent rule boils down the complex task of creating a sustainable retirement income stream to just one number and three steps.

1 Withdraw 4 percent of your total retirement assets as income in your first year of retirement.
2 In year two, increase last year's income by the rate of inflation and use that as your new yearly income amount.
3 Repeat Step Two to fund each future year of retirement.

Imagine you enter retirement with a portfolio of $1 million. According to this rule, you should

PRO TIP

Consider taking a flexible approach to your withdrawal rate that's based on market performance and the stage of retirement you're in.

withdraw 4 percent of that balance, or $40,000, to use for expenses in your first year as a retiree. If inflation is 2.5 percent in year two, you would increase your yearly withdrawal by 2.5 percent, to $41,000. That way, you'll have the same purchasing power as the previous year. If inflation clocks in at 3 percent in year three, your withdrawal should go up to $42,230 ($41,000 × 1.03).

Doubts Emerging

Since its introduction, the 4 percent rule has been embraced for its ease and specificity. But these days, many experts are voicing serious doubts about whether the 4 percent rule is still appropriate. Interest rates may be rising, but they're still very low by historical standards. That fact could spell trouble for retirees who depend heavily on yields from bonds and other fixed-income investments. Couple that with the fact that retirements are extending as Americans' life expectancy is rising, and 4 percent may be too aggressive to ensure today's retirees won't outlive their savings.

Other Income-Withdrawal Strategies

A flexible approach to withdrawals can provide an appropriate income level and help ensure that you don't outlive your savings. In recent years, retirement experts have devised alternative strategies that begin with a 5 percent withdrawal rate, then modify that figure based on market performance. By basing your retirement income partly on investment returns, you can rest assured you're not blowing through your savings—and maybe afford to live a little larger in the process. Here are two options to consider:

The Erase-Inflation Method This one keeps it simple. All you do is skip inflation adjustment after any year in which your retirement investments decline in value. Let's say, during your

The 4 percent rule is a well-known withdrawal method— but is it right for you?

first year of retirement, inflation is 2.5 percent, but a down year in the stock market trims 6 percent off your retirement balance. Under the 4 percent rule, you'd ignore the 6 percent loss and increase next year's withdrawal 2.5 percent to follow inflation.

But with the erase-inflation method, the 6 percent loss means you leave your income level constant for the year—as if inflation were 0 percent. This method effectively lowers the purchasing power of your retirement income as a consequence of down-market years. It also affords you a little more income in your early retirement years than the 4 percent rule, as experts found a starting withdrawal rate of 5 percent consistently succeeds over a 30-year span.

The Guardrail Method Similar to the erase-inflation method, the guardrail method also has you start withdrawals at 5 percent and forgo inflation increases in down years. However, the guardrail method adds another market-dependent layer to the equation, ensuring that your withdrawals stay between a guardrail of 4 to 6 percent of your total retirement savings. If your previous year's withdrawal represents more than 6 percent of your total savings, you would reduce your withdrawal amount by 10 percent this year to get back on course. Meanwhile, if the previous year's withdrawal represents less than 4 percent of your total savings, you would increase your withdrawal by 10 percent this year. (Any year your withdrawal falls within 4 percent and 6 percent, all you have to do is check whether your investments generated a positive return, and adjust for inflation if they did.)

For example, say you enter retirement with $1,500,000, giving you $75,000 in your first year, based on a 5 percent withdrawal rate. Each year after that, determine what percentage of your total portfolio your withdrawal represents.

PRO TIP

Plan to reassess your goals and lifestyle at least annually in retirement—and shift your withdrawal strategy accordingly.

After two years, say you have taken a total of $150,000 ($75,000 × 2) out of your portfolio. Your remaining balance is $1,350,000. Imagine the market dives at the same time, pulling your balance down to $1,200,000.

At this point, your $75,000 withdrawal would represent 6.25 percent of your total

savings ($75,000/$1,200,000)—above the 6 percent cap specified by the guardrail method. As a result, you should lower your "salary" by 10 percent (or $7,500), and withdraw only $67,500 over the next year.

The flip side of this method is that you can give yourself a 10 percent raise any year in which the ratio falls below 4 percent, giving you a nice boost in cash flow during years when the stock market grows your nest egg enough.

Considerations for Early Retirees

More-sophisticated withdrawal patterns like these are a great way to factor market performance into your retirement strategy. But the question of adequate income is still tricky for early retirees.

Since the time you spend in retirement will likely be long, you may need to pull money from your savings at a more conservative rate to make your investments last. You might counter that issue, however, if you're able to lean on revenue from a rental property or other passive income stream.

Another complication is the often-wide variation in spending levels in different stages of an early retiree's future. For instance, you may be happy with an income well below 4 percent or 5 percent of your portfolio a decade or two into retirement, if it affords you more money to spend up front during the early years. Considering the drastic changes a person's lifestyle can go through over the course of 40 or more years, there's little chance that maintaining the same general income level each and every year will make practical sense.

That's why for the majority of retirees, it's best to sit down once a year to revisit your goals and

Most retirees need more income at some stages of retirement than others.

consider life changes that may cause you to shift your retirement income schedule accordingly. The longer you expect to spend in retirement, the more important it is to adopt a dynamic approach to income withdrawals. But that doesn't mean you should view the 4 percent rule or any other "set it and forget it" approach as useless. Instead, consider using the 4 percent rule as a starting point. Calculate what income 4 percent of your retirement balance would create and how close that amount is to funding your desired lifestyle. If it strikes you as too low, take a closer look at one of the market-adjusted options that may let you withdraw more early on.

During this annual reassessment, revisit other personal factors that help drive your planning.

- How long do you hope to live in retirement?
- How important are Social Security, pensions and other fixed-revenue streams?
- Are any health issues likely to cause your medical costs to fluctuate later on?

For many, the answers to these questions will change, becoming clearer as retirement progresses. By continually honing an income system that evolves with your needs, you can get the most out of early retirement and position yourself for financial success in the long run. ∎

159

Understanding Required Minimum Distributions
The Rules of Withdrawals and How They Can Impact Your Investments

Since contributions to traditional retirement accounts are not taxed as income when you put money in the account, you are not required to pay taxes on it right away.

However, the IRS will collect taxes eventually. That's why, most years, you must begin taking required minimum distributions (RMDs) from qualifying accounts when you reach age 72. There are exceptions: In 2020, for example, RMDs were waived as part of the national economic stimulus after the COVID-19 pandemic. Visit irs.gov for the status of RMDs in 2021 and beyond.

Not all retirement accounts have RMDs, so it's important to know which accounts require them and how much you need to withdraw and when.

Accounts With RMDs
- Traditional IRAs
- SEP and SIMPLE IRAs
- Traditional and Roth 401(k) plans
- All other employer-sponsored plans, including profit-sharing, 403(b) and 457(b) plans

Accounts Without RMDs
- Roth IRAs

How to Handle Distributions

There are several rules that affect your distributions. How much you must withdraw is calculated using the IRS' Uniform Lifetime Table. At age 70, the standard divisor is 27.4, which calculates a rate of 3.65 percent (age divided by divisor) for your first RMD. At age 71, the divisor is 26.5, and the required percentage of your portfolio rises to 3.77 percent. Each year, the divisor decreases slightly, so you're required to withdraw a larger portion of your savings as you age. You must calculate the RMD separately for each qualified account based on the value of the account on December 31 of the previous year.

You'll also need to be aware of when you can withdraw. Typically, you must take your first

RMD by April 1 of the year after you turn 70½. Even if you turned 70½ in December 2019, for example, you would have had to take your first RMD by April 1, 2020. Then you'd need to take subsequent RMDs before December 31, 2020. In a scenario like this, it may be wise to take the first RMD in December of the year you turn 70½ and the following RMD the year after, so you're not making two large withdrawals in the same calendar year. After the first two years, there will be no overlap in the time line on when to withdraw.

Lastly, consider how you'll collect your distributions. You can take your RMD as a lump sum, or you can choose an automatic monthly withdrawal. Those who opt to receive a lump sum typically liquidate the distribution and reinvest most of it. Each year, you can adjust your strategy based on your situation.

There is an exception to these rules. If your spouse is more than 10 years younger than you and is your only beneficiary, the IRS allows you to use a larger divisor, which decreases the amount of your RMD and allows more money to stay in your account. If at any time you don't take RMDs, or if the distributions are not large enough, you may have to pay a 50 percent excise tax on the amount your distribution would have been, had you taken it as required. These guidelines remain in flux, however, so make sure to check the IRS website for up-to-date information. ■

Learning the rules about RMDs now helps you plan for the future.

Different types of investment accounts are treated differently at tax time.

Paying Taxes on Retirement Income
What You Need to Know Before You Retire

No matter when you decide to retire, you'll likely be pulling from several sources of income to get through your post-work years. Be aware that each type of investment account has different taxation rules. For example, withdrawals from brokerage accounts are taxed at capital gains rates, distributions from traditional IRAs are taxed as ordinary income, and distributions from Roth IRAs are exempt from taxes. And Social Security has specific rules, too.

PRO TIP

Since Roth IRAs are the only retirement account that offers tax-free withdrawals, try to withdraw from them last, so your tax-free savings can grow.

To accurately plan your retirement, you'll need to know how much you owe Uncle Sam, when you are required to make withdrawals and the impact taxes on distributions may have on your goals. Here's a breakdown of the most common sources of retirement income and what you need to know about how they're taxed.

Traditional IRA, Traditional 401(k) and Roth 401(k) Accounts

Your withdrawals from traditional tax-deferred retirement accounts are taxed at your normal income tax rate, which can really throw off your cash flow if you're not prepared. You'll need to start taking required minimum distributions by the time you reach the age of 70½, so plan accordingly, using your income tax rate as a guide to estimate how much you'll owe. Roth 401(k) accounts also require minimum distributions, though you can defer them past the age of 70½ if you are still working.

Roth IRAs

A Roth IRA is the only true tax-free account available, so take advantage of it by opening one early. These accounts do not have RMDs like traditional IRAs, but you must be over the age of 59½—and must have had the account open for at least five years—before you start pulling your money out in order to avoid early-withdrawal penalties. As a general rule of thumb, it's smart to draw from this account last, to allow as much time as possible for your tax-free savings to grow.

Taxable Investments

Profits from the sale of stocks, bonds and real estate that you hold outside of tax-advantaged retirement accounts are taxed at capital gains rates, which vary depending on how long you've owned the investments. Short-term capital gains apply to investments you've owned less than one year and are taxed at your ordinary income tax rate. Long-term investments are subject to capital-gains rates based on your tax bracket; those rates are 0 percent, 15 percent or 20 percent. Luckily, some—or all—of the profits from selling your primary residence are exempt from capital-gains tax, so long as you've lived in the house for two of the five years prior to the sale. If you're single, you don't pay capital gains on the first $250,000 you make in profits; if you're married and file jointly, you receive a $500,000 exemption.

Other investments, such as interest on your savings accounts and CDs, are taxed at your ordinary income rate.

Social Security

Many retirees rely on Social Security benefits, but not everyone is aware that these benefits can be taxed. The tax rate depends on your provisional income (the sum of your adjusted gross income, any tax-free interest from other investments and 50 percent of your benefits). Expect to pay taxes if your provisional income exceeds $25,000 on an individual tax return or $32,000 on a joint tax return. No matter how much your provisional income is, you'll never have to pay taxes on more than 85 percent of your Social Security benefits.

Different types of investments are subject to different tax rates.

Pensions

Some employees receive a pension as part of their retirement benefits. Assuming you made no after-tax contributions to the plan, payments from private and government pensions are typically taxed at your ordinary income rate.

Annuities

Annuities are typically purchased with income that's already been taxed, and then issue payments over time. The portion of the payment representing your principal is tax-free, while you'll pay taxes on any investment growth. Conversely, if you purchased the annuity with pretax funds, such as from a traditional IRA, your entire payment will be taxed as ordinary income.

Withdrawal Order

Consider making withdrawals in this sequence.

1 RMDs from traditional IRA, traditional 401(k) and Roth 401(k) accounts
2 Taxable accounts
3 Additional withdrawals from tax-deferred accounts, including your traditional IRA and 401(k) accounts
4 Roth IRAs and additional withdrawals from Roth 401(k) accounts

Making withdrawals in this order allows you to keep your money in tax-exempt accounts the longest, to allow for the greatest returns and even the possibility that you can pass some tax-advantaged assets on to the next generation. ■

An annuity can help even
out your income, in early
retirement and beyond.

Financial Worksheets

Use these pages to plan your
early retirement and track your progress

08 | **WISH LIST** | 01 | 02 | 03 | 04 | 05 | 06 | 07 | 08 | 09 | 10 | 11 | 12 | 13 | 14 | 15

Retirement Lifestyle Wish List

Everyone has a different vision of their ideal retirement. Complete this worksheet to flesh out your ideas of retirement, and use it as a guide for making your vision a reality.

Where do you want to live? Where you are now or somewhere else? In the city or in the country? In the U.S. or abroad? Near the ocean or in the mountains?

_____
_____
_____

What type of living situation do you envision? Are you interested in downsizing? Owning or renting?

_____
_____

How often would you prefer to see your family and close friends? Which people are especially important for you to be in close contact with?

_____
_____
_____

What passions do you want to pursue?

_____
_____

What hobbies are you interested in trying out?

_____

What do you want to learn more about?

_____

Where do you want to travel? How frequently do you want to go on trips?

_____
_____

Do you want to volunteer? For what types of organizations and in what capacity?

_____
_____

Are you interested in part-time work? What type?

_____
_____

What will your sources of income be?

_____

Map out what you want your retirement years to look like.

169

08 RELOCATING 01 | 02 | 03 | 04 | 05 | 06 | 07 | 08 | 09 | 10 | 11 | 12 | 13 | 14 | 15

Calculate the Costs of Relocating

Housing costs aren't the only expenses to consider when you're planning to move in retirement. Even if you're downsizing, you'll have to spend money on the move itself. And depending on where you live and where you're going, you might end up spending more on living expenses in your new location than you do now. Consider the following costs before you move.

Costs of Moving

Expenses

Moving Van or Professional Movers	$
Packing Materials	$
Moving Insurance	$
Travel Costs	$
Shipping Fees	$
Storage Unit Rental	$
Nights in Hotel or Other Short-Term Housing	$
Utility Balances and Deposits	$
New Furniture and Appliances	$
TOTAL	$

Costs of Living (Monthly)

	Current Home	New Home (Estimated)	Difference
Mortgage or Rent	$	$	$
Utilities	$	$	$
Taxes	$	$	$
Groceries	$	$	$
Transportation	$	$	$
Health Insurance	$	$	$
Car Insurance	$	$	$
Homeowners Insurance	$	$	$
TOTAL			$

Downsizing Checklist

Whether you're moving to a smaller home or want to create new space in your current home, you'll have to start by taking stock of all of the items, large and small, you've accumulated over the years. Follow these steps to minimize stress when you downsize.

Keep   Sell   Donate   Recycle

1 Organize Your Stuff Go through all the items you own and sort them into four categories: Keep, give away to friends/family, donate or sell. Make sure to include anything stored away in your garage or attic. If you're moving to a new home, start packing the things you intend to keep.

2 Sell What You Can You have a few options for trying to sell unwanted items. A garage or yard sale is a great way to find buyers for miscellaneous small objects you may have collected over the years. Consider Craigslist, eBay or Nextdoor for larger appliances and furniture. And for books and clothes, inquire if local stores and consignment shops will resell them and give you a cut of the proceeds.

3 Give Away and Donate Next, give away the items you've set aside for family and friends, and donate whatever else may be left and is in good shape to charities. In addition to national nonprofits, local organizations like homeless shelters and refugee-assistance organizations are often in need of furniture, clothes and other items.

4 Recycle or Throw Away Whatever's Left Check your local ordinances to see what items you can leave on your curb for recycling and trash pickup, and what you need to deliver to a nearby dump or transfer center yourself. If you have an especially large amount of trash, consider renting a dumpster or hiring a trash-removal service.

08 | **EXPENSES** | 01 | 02 | 03 | 04 | 05 | 06 | 07 | 08 | 09 | 10 | 11 | 12 | 13 | 14 | 15

Current and Retirement Expenses Worksheet

As you plan for early retirement, it can help to look at current spending as well as forecast what your future expenses might look like. Use this worksheet to track expenses now and estimate what your fixed and discretionary costs will be in retirement. This can also illuminate areas where you could immediately reduce spending, potentially enabling you to retire even sooner.

HOUSING

	Monthly Cost Now	Monthly Cost in Retirement
Mortgage Payment/Rent	$	$
Property Taxes	$	$
Homeowners Insurance	$	$
Electricity	$	$
Heating Oil/Gas	$	$
Water	$	$
Trash	$	$
Sewer	$	$
Telephone	$	$
Cellphone	$	$
Cable/Internet	$	$
Other	$	$

TRANSPORTATION

	Monthly Cost Now	Monthly Cost in Retirement
Auto Payment	$	$
Auto Insurance	$	$
License/Registration/Excise Tax	$	$
Fuel	$	$
Repairs	$	$
Public Transportation	$	$
Other	$	$

MEDICAL & HEALTH

Monthly Cost Now

Monthly Cost in Retirement

Health Insurance $ $

Life Insurance $ $

Long-Term-Care Insurance $ $

Disability Insurance $ $

Out-of-Pocket Medical Expenses $ $

Out-of-Pocket Dental Expenses $ $

Other $ $

INCOME TAXES

Monthly Cost Now

Monthly Cost in Retirement

Federal Taxes $ $

State Taxes $ $

Local Taxes $ $

OTHER ESSENTIALS

Monthly Cost Now

Monthly Cost in Retirement

Groceries $ $

Clothing $ $

Personal-Care Products $ $

Other $ $

DISCRETIONARY SPENDING

Monthly Cost Now

Monthly Cost in Retirement

Dining Out/Coffee $ $

Subscriptions/Apps $ $

Travel $ $

Gifts & Charitable Donations $ $

Gym Memberships/Classes $ $

Education $ $

Entertainment $ $

Hobbies $ $

Hair/Beauty Appointments $ $

Other $ $

TOTALS

Monthly Cost Now

Monthly Cost in Retirement

$ $

Determine your income sources so you can savor your time in retirement.

Planning Your Income Sources in Retirement

In order to pull the plug on your day job, you'll want a healthy sense of confidence that you can bring in enough income to meet or exceed your expenses. Use this worksheet to track the income you expect to bring in during the early part of your retirement. Then add the sources of income that will kick in during your later years. See how the numbers work out, and perhaps even get inspired to create additional streams of income.

Early Retirement

Income Sources	Monthly	Annual
Rent From Investment Properties (or Airbnb)	$	$
Pension	$	$
Savings Account/CDs	$	$
Side Hustle/Part-Time Job	$	$
Stock Dividends	$	$
Other	$	$

Late Retirement

Income Sources	Monthly	Annual
Social Security	$	$
Retirement-Plan Withdrawals	$	$
Annuity Payment	$	$
Other	$	$

	Early Income Retirement	Income in Retirement
TOTALS	$	$

175

Debt Payoff

One of the quickest ways to free up extra money so you can reach early retirement is to kill your debt. The first step: getting real about how much debt you have. Use this worksheet to list all your debt—including your mortgage, credit cards, home equity and auto loans, and student debt.

Then decide how you'll tackle it. Aim to pay the minimum on all your debts except for one. Put

extra money toward that targeted debt. Then, once you've paid it off, you can roll that payment into the next debt on your list.

You'll pay less in interest over time if you focus on paying off the highest-interest debt first. But you may find it inspiring to immediately knock off the debt with the lowest dollar amount, giving you a quick win and the drive to keep going.

DEBT	Interest Rate	Loan Balance	Monthly Minimum Payment	Extra Payment	Date Paid Off
	%	$	$	$	
	%	$	$	$	
	%	$	$	$	
	%	$	$	$	
	%	$	$	$	
	%	$	$	$	
	%	$	$	$	
	%	$	$	$	
	%	$	$	$	
	%	$	$	$	
	%	$	$	$	
	%	$	$	$	
	%	$	$	$	
	%	$	$	$	
	%	$	$	$	
	%	$	$	$	
	%	$	$	$	

Calculate Your RMD

You must begin withdrawing your required minimum distribution (RMD) from your retirement account by the year you turn 72. The deadline for receiving your RMD the year you turn 72 is April 1. For all subsequent years, the deadline is December 31.

The amount of your RMD is determined by dividing the retirement account balance as of December 31 of the previous year by your life expectancy factor, which is predetermined by the IRS. Use this chart below to calculate the amount you'll need to withdraw.

Your RMD

IRA balance on December 31 of the previous year

$ _____

Distribution period from the table below for your age on your birthday this year

$ _____

Your balance divided by your life expectancy factor

$ _____

Age	Life Expectancy Factor	Age	Life Expectancy Factor	Age	Life Expectancy Factor	Age	Life Expectancy Factor
70	27.4	82	17.1	94	9.1	106	4.2
71	26.5	83	16.3	95	8.6	107	3.9
72	25.6	84	15.5	96	8.1	108	3.7
73	24.7	85	14.8	97	7.6	109	3.4
74	23.8	86	14.1	98	7.1	110	3.1
75	22.9	87	13.4	99	6.7	111	2.9
76	22.0	88	12.7	100	6.3	112	2.6
77	21.2	89	12.0	101	5.9	113	2.4
78	20.3	90	11.4	102	5.5	114	2.1
79	19.5	91	10.8	103	5.2	115+	1.9
80	18.7	92	10.2	104	4.9		
81	17.9	93	9.6	105	4.5		

08 | **HEALTH CARE COSTS** | 01 | 02 | 03 | 04 | 05 | 06 | 07 | 08 | 09 | 10 | 11 | 12 | 13 | 14 | 15

Estimate Your Health Care Costs

You can't predict what your health care needs will be, but you can prepare for monthly premiums, deductibles and copays. As you consider how to structure your Medicare coverage, compare plans by thinking about your out-of-pocket costs in various scenarios.

Compare Potential Expenses Under Various Plans

Possible Costs	Plan No. 1	Plan No. 2	Plan No. 3
Monthly Premium (including drug coverage and any supplemental insurance)	$	$	$
Annual (or benefit period) Deductible	$	$	$
Yearly Cap on Out-of-Pocket Expenses, If Any	$	$	$
Coinsurance Rate for Inpatient Care	$	$	$
Out-of-Pocket Costs for Surgery and Hospital Stay With a Total Bill of $30,000	$	$	$
Out-of-Pocket Costs for Doctor's Visit for Diagnostic Tests Totaling $3,000	$	$	$

Medicare Cheat Sheet

You may not yet be eligible for Medicare, the federal health-insurance program for those 65 and older. But it's worth taking a little time now to familiarize yourself with the basics so that you'll be ready when it's time to apply.

Eligibility You become eligible for Medicare on the day you turn 65. If you're already receiving Social Security benefits, you'll be automatically enrolled in Parts A and B; otherwise, you must enroll online, on the phone or in person.

Enrollment Medicare offers limited windows for enrollment. The Initial Enrollment Period (IEP) spans from three months before the month you turn 65 to three months after the month you turn 65. Missing the IEP could bring late-enrollment penalties, higher premiums and gaps in your health care coverage.

> **Medicare Parts A–D** The Medicare program is divided into several parts, each of which provides different kinds of coverage for different costs (or, in some cases, for no cost at all).

Medigap Insurance, also known as Medicare supplemental insurance, fills some of the gaps that exist in the Medicare program. Medigap insurance is purchased through private insurers instead of through Medicare, and premiums vary significantly.

PART A

Covers hospital services like inpatient stays, care in a skilled nursing facility, hospice care and sometimes home health care. Part A coverage is free, so long as you (or your spouse) paid Medicare payroll taxes for at least 10 years. Once you meet the annual deductible, Part A typically covers 100 percent of the hospitalization costs for up to 60 days.

PART B

Covers visits to a doctor's office and other outpatient services. In 2020, the Part B base monthly premium was $144.60, though higher earners may pay as much as $5,000 a year. After meeting the annual deductible, Part B will cover 80 percent of approved costs. Visit cms.gov for the most current information.

PART C

(Also called Medicare Advantage) provides health care coverage through private insurance companies. Part C plans include the same coverage as traditional Medicare Parts A and B, and it may also include additional vision, hearing and dental benefits and/or prescription drug coverage. The National Association on Aging estimates the average Part C premium costs to be $28 per month, though it can vary.

PART D

Pays for prescription drugs. The basic monthly premium for Part D coverage in 2020 was just over $42. Part D plans can vary quite a bit in terms of which drugs they cover and at what cost. Before picking a Part D plan, make sure to check how much you'll be paying to get your current medications.

FOR MORE INFORMATION, VISIT MEDICARE.GOV

Medicare Enrollment Checklist

Ready to sign up? Follow these steps to get the coverage you need in a timely manner. For more information, go to medicare.gov.

☑ Know When to Enroll

Your initial seven-month enrollment period begins three months before your 65th birthday. By signing up before you turn 65, you can ensure that your coverage will kick in as soon as you are eligible to receive benefits. However, if you still have health benefits coverage through an employer (yours or your spouse's), you may want to delay enrolling until that coverage ends. If you missed your initial enrollment period, mark your calendar for the next general enrollment period.

☑ Compare Original Medicare and Part C

Part C plans, also known as Medicare Advantage (MA) plans, are sold by private insurers. They can offer more extensive benefits than Original Medicare, but they limit where you can get your care. Use Medicare's Plan Finder (medicare.gov/find-a-plan) to see which MA plans are available in your area, and compare their costs to those of Original Medicare.

☑ Gather Documents

To apply for Medicare, you'll need your Social Security number, original birth certificate and legal residency documents, as well as your original marriage certificate if you're married. If you've delayed signing up for Part B, you'll also need proof of your employer-sponsored insurance policy.

☑ Enroll

You will be automatically enrolled in Original Medicare when you turn 65 years old if you have been collecting Social Security benefits for at least four months. In this case, your premium will be deducted from your first benefits check. If you are not automatically enrolled, you'll need to apply online, over the phone or in person.

☑ Get Supplemental Coverage

If you are opting for Original Medicare and want to add on prescription drug coverage, use Medicare's online Plan Finder to locate a Part D plan that best works for you. You can also use this tool to locate a Medigap insurance policy, if you think that you want or need one. If you've decided to go with Part C coverage instead, contact the insurance company during your Initial Enrollment Period so you don't have to wait until the open enrollment period to join the plan. Not all MA plans are designed to include prescription drug coverage, so if yours doesn't, make sure to sign up for a Part D plan separately.

Prescription Drug List

Keep track of which drugs you're taking and how much they cost. Save this worksheet for the next time you decide to check out your options in the Medicare Plan Finder.

My Prescriptions	Covered By My Plan?	Monthly Cost
		$
		$
		$
		$
		$
		$
		$
		$
		$
		$
		$
		$
		$
		$
		$
		$
		$
		$
		$
		$
		$
		$

Supplementing Medicare With an HSA

Instead of cashing out of your health savings account (HSA), learn how to use it to cash in. The balance in your HSA could become more useful after you choose a Medicare plan. Just remember to plan ahead so your balance is as large as possible: Once you sign up for Medicare, you can only take money out of your HSA; you won't be able to put any more in. Fill in the list below and keep it with your important financial papers, and then keep your coverage information handy in your wallet, along with your Medicare ID card.

HSA Account Details

Provider Name

_____

_____

Provider Phone

_____

_____

Account Login/Password

_____

_____

Account Number

_____

Covered Family Members

_____

_____

_____

When Medicare Doesn't Cover These Costs, Your HSA Covers:

- ☑ The prevention, diagnosis, treatment and cure of any illness or defect in any function of the body
- ☑ Over-the-counter medications for which you receive a prescription
- ☑ Prescription drugs
- ☑ Transport to medical care
- ☑ Insulin medication
- ☑ Medicare or Medicare Advantage premiums
- ☑ Any deductibles
- ☑ Copayments or coinsurance payments

Your HSA Doesn't Cover:

- ☒ Over-the-counter drugs and medicines for which you don't receive a prescription
- ☒ Costs to support overall health, like vitamins, a gym membership or a vacation
- ☒ Medigap premiums

Estate Planning

Let's face it—estate planning is considerably less fun than planning for early retirement. But creating a plan for your assets after you die can have a huge impact, both financially and emotionally, on your heirs. Use this checklist to track your progress in creating a thorough estate plan.

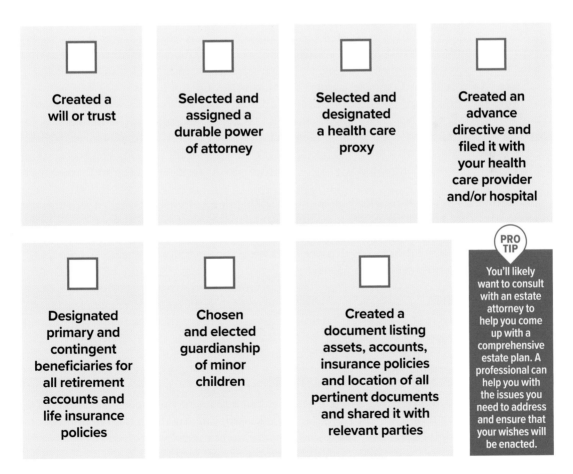

☐ Created a will or trust

☐ Selected and assigned a durable power of attorney

☐ Selected and designated a health care proxy

☐ Created an advance directive and filed it with your health care provider and/or hospital

☐ Designated primary and contingent beneficiaries for all retirement accounts and life insurance policies

☐ Chosen and elected guardianship of minor children

☐ Created a document listing assets, accounts, insurance policies and location of all pertinent documents and shared it with relevant parties

PRO TIP

You'll likely want to consult with an estate attorney to help you come up with a comprehensive estate plan. A professional can help you with the issues you need to address and ensure that your wishes will be enacted.

What to Look for in a Long-Term-Care Facility

If you or your loved one is considering moving into a long-term-care facility, it's important to do your homework first. After all, you're not just choosing a building; you're choosing a new home. Here's a rundown of what to look for.

✅ **A Highly Ranked Facility** Start by searching for facilities online. At medicare.gov, you can find a "Nursing Home Compare" database that ranks facilities based on recent inspection documents. ProPublica's "Nursing Home Inspect" offers similar evaluations using even more detailed data. Narrow your search to facilities that receive high rankings.

✅ **Location** Many people benefit from living in a long-term-care facility that is close to family and friends to make visiting more convenient. Also consider whether you want to live in a busy part of a city, a more rural setting or somewhere in between.

✅ **Size** If you're more social, a larger facility may provide more opportunities for interaction with other people. If quiet and solitude is more your thing, consider a smaller facility.

✅ **Experienced and Well-Regarded Staff** The staff of a long-term-care facility is an essential component of residents' day-to-day lives. Ask about the experience of the facility's employees, and whether they have opportunities for continuing education and training programs. Look for a turnover rate of less than 30 percent.

✅ **An On-Site Nurse** Immediate medical support is a huge plus in a long-term-care facility. Look for a home with an on-site registered nurse, or at least one in which an RN is available most of the day.

✅ **A Clean and Calm Environment** Visit facilities you're interested in to get a feel for them. Is the building clean? Is there a sense of calm and order? Do the residents appear well-cared-for?

✅ **Regular Activities** Scheduled activities add stimulation to those who live there. Check to see if the facility schedules movies, lectures, concerts, group meetings or other entertainment.

✅ **Good Food** Are there multiple options at every meal? Is the food well-prepared and tasty? And is the dining area a pleasant environment that is conducive to enjoying both your meals and the company of fellow diners?

✅ **Price** While you want to choose the facility that best meets your needs, you also need to make sure you can afford it for many years to come. Don't neglect your budget as you search for the perfect facility.

Early-Retirement Resources

Achieving early retirement takes consistency and commitment, but a regular dash of inspiration helps, too. Here is a list of podcasts, apps and websites to keep you fueled on your quest for early retirement.

PODCASTS

• **Afford Anything** Blogger Paula Pant offers up advice to her guests on how to leave the conventional 9-to-5 workplace behind and support yourself through investments. affordanything.com

• **Choose FI** Hosts Brad Barrett and Jonathan Mendonsa weigh in on how to save more and achieve financial independence. choosefi.com/all-podcast-episodes

• **The FI Show** Hosts Cody Berman and Justin Taylor talk financial independence, investing, innovation and more with a friendly, informal take on finance. thefishow.com

• **Frugal Friends Podcast** Hosts (and galpals) Jen Smith and Jill Sirianni offer advice on how to set a budget, pay off debt and gain control over your money. frugalfriendspodcast.com

• **So Money** Author and financial correspondent Farnoosh Torabi talks money with top business minds, authors and influencers. podcast.farnoosh.tv

APPS

• **Digit** The online savings account uses its own algorithms to determine when you should save versus spend. Check website for pricing; digit.co

• **Mint** Put all your finances in one place, from bank accounts and credit cards to retirement savings and more. Free; mint.com

• **Personal Capital** Retirement planning is just one easy-to-access feature in this financial management app. Free, fee for managing assets; personalcapital.com

• **Wealthfront** Direct-deposit your paycheck with the app and it will automatically split into usages like emergency funds, bill payments, investments and more. Free, fee for managing assets; wealthfront.com

• **YNAB** Use it to predetermine your expenses so you can better manage your money. Check website for pricing; youneedabudget.com

BLOGS & FORUMS

1500 Days to Freedom
1500days.com

Budgets Are Sexy
budgetsaresexy.com

Early-Retirement.org
early-retirement.org

Frugalwoods
frugalwoods.com

Get Rich Slowly
getrichslowly.org

Mad Fientist
madfientist.com

Mr. Money Mustache
mrmoney-mustache.com

Our Next Life
ournextlife.com

Reddit FI/RE forum
reddit.com/r/financial-independence

Retire by 40
retireby40.org

Think Save Retire
thinksaveretire.com

CREDITS

COVER Aleksandr Elesin **2-3** Blend Images RM/Getty Images **4-5** Jupiterimages/Getty Images; Tinpixels/Getty Images; Sorbetto/Getty Images **6-7** Compassionate Eye Foundation/Andrew Olney/Getty Images **8-9** Caiaimage/Getty Images **10-11** Rana Faure/Corbis/VCG/Getty Images **12-13** Ariel Skelley/Getty Images **14-15** Ariel Skelley/Getty Images **16-17** Hybrid Images/Getty Images **18-19** Hero Images/Getty Images; TarikVision/Shutterstock **20-21** Westend61/Getty Images **22-23** Jupiterimages/Getty Images **24-25** Ariel Skelley/Getty Images **26-27** TarikVision/Shutterstock; PeopleImages/Getty Images **28-29** Henglein and Steets/Getty Images **30-31** terng99/Shutterstock **32-33** Hero Images/Getty Images **34-35** shapecharge/Getty Images **36-37** sylv1rob1/Shutterstock **38-39** Caiaimage/Shutterstock **40-41** svetikd/Getty Images **42-43** Westend61/Getty Images **44-45** Blend Images/Getty Images **46-47** yenwen/Getty Images **48-49** Mike Albright Photography/Shutterstock; welcomia/Shutterstock; Sean Pavone/Shutterstock; CK Foto/Shutterstock; Fotoluminate LLC/Shutterstock **50-51** Dr. Victor Wong/Shutterstock; pisaphotography/Shutterstock; WikiMedia Commons; Sean Pavone/Shutterstock; S.Borisov/Shutterstock **52-53** IP Galanternik D.U./Getty Images **54-55** Getty Images **56-57** MoMo Productions/Getty Images **58-59** Sorbetto/Getty Images **60-61** Andy Dean Photography/Shutterstock **62-63** Maskot/Getty Images; Klaus Vedfelt/Getty Images **64-65** Ariel Skelley/Getty Images; Lucien Freud/Shutterstock **66-67** EyeEm/Getty Images **68-69** Cavan Images/Getty Images **70-71** GoodStudio/Shutterstock **72-73** Andrey_Popov/Shutterstock **74-75** Rawpixel.com/Shutterstock **76-77** GoodStudio/Shutterstock **78-79** Trikona/Shutterstock **80-81** Fred Froese/Getty Images **82-83** Cecilie_Arcurs/Getty Images **84-85** Westend61/Getty Images **86-87** robuart/Shutterstock **88-89** sorbetto/Getty Images **90-91** Geber86/Getty Images **92-93** Brian Hagiwara/Shutterstock **94-95** FabrikaSimf/Shutterstock **96-97** Anthony Bradshaw/Getty Images **98-99** Geber86/Getty Images **100-101** Martin Poole/Getty Images **102-103** Jeffrey Hamilton/Getty Images **104-105** Marc Romanelli/Getty Images **106-107** Don Mason/Getty Images **108-109** John M Lund Photography Inc/Getty Images **110-111** TZIDO SUN/Shutterstock **112-113** solar22/Shutterstock **114-115** Chris Clor/Getty Images **116-117** Peter Dazeley/Getty Images **118-119** Caiaimage/Getty Images **120-121** Andy Roberts/Getty Images **122-123** EyeEm/Getty Images **124-125** Getty Images; Comstock Images/Getty Images **126-127** Tay Junior/Getty Images **128-129** Tinpixels/Getty Images **130-131** Viktoria Kurpas/Shutterstock **132-133** JGI/Jamie Grill/Getty Images **134-135** Getty Images **136-137** EyeEm/Getty Images **138-139** Dim Tik/Shutterstock **140-141** Stmool/Shutterstock; polymanu/Shutterstock **142-143** Blend Images/Getty Images **144-145** Blend Images/Getty Images **146-147** Photon photo/Shutterstock **148-149** Andersen Ross Photography Inc/Getty Images; Mascha Tace/Shutterstock **150-151** Rawpixel.com/Shutterstock **152-153** Tetra Images/Getty Images **154-155** sorbetto/Getty Images; Ivelin Radkov/Shutterstock **156-157** Andrey_Popov/Shutterstock **158-159** JAG IMAGES/Getty Images **160-161** Getty Images **162-163** Rawpixel.com/Shutterstock **164-165** TrifonenkoIvan/Shutterstock **166-167** siridhata/Shutterstock **168-169** Vesnaandjic/Getty Images **174-175** David Jakle/Getty Images **BACK COVER** DNY59/Getty Images; katleho Seisa/Getty Images; shapecharge/Getty Images

SPECIAL THANKS TO CONTRIBUTING WRITERS

ERIN HEGER

ANDREW PALMER

PARAM ANAND SINGH

CENTENNIAL BOOKS

An Imprint of
Centennial Media, LLC
40 Worth St., 10th Floor
New York, NY 10013, U.S.A.

ISBN 978-1-951274-49-8

Distributed by
Simon & Schuster, Inc.
1230 Avenue of the Americas
New York, NY 10020, U.S.A.

For information about custom editions, special sales and premium and corporate purchases,
please contact Centennial Media at contact@centennialmedia.com.

Manufactured in China

Publishers & Co-Founders Ben Harris, Sebastian Raatz
Editorial Director Annabel Vered
Creative Director Jessica Power
Executive Editor Janet Giovanelli
Deputy Editors Ron Kelly, Alyssa Shaffer
Design Director Martin Elfers
Senior Art Director Pino Impastato
Art Directors Olga Jakim, Natali Suasnavas, Joseph Ulatowski
Copy/Production Patty Carroll, Angela Taormina
Assistant Art Director Jaclyn Loney
Photo Editor Jenny Veiga
Production Manager Paul Rodina
Production Assistant Alyssa Swiderski
Editorial Assistant Tiana Schippa
Sales & Marketing Jeremy Nurnberg